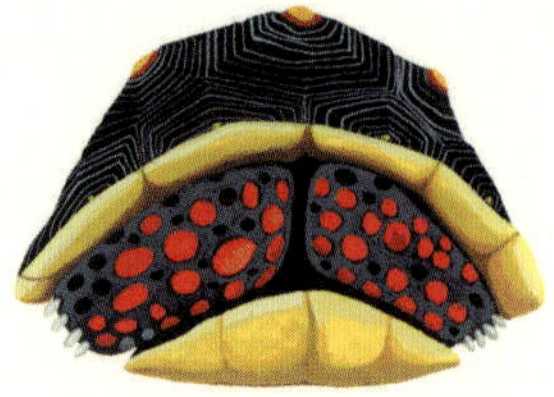

Published in the UK in 2025 by Post Wave Children's Books,
an imprint of Post Wave Publishing UK Ltd,
Runway East, 24-28 Bloomsbury Way, London, WC1A 2SN
www.postwavepublishing.com

A catalogue record of this book is available from the British Library.

First edition 2022, published with permission of Editorial Amanuta Limitada
Original title: *Agua y Tierra: Anfibios y reptiles de América*
Text copyright © 2022 Martha Crump and Andrés Charrier
Illustration copyright © 2022 Loreto Salinas
Design copyright © 2022 by Editorial Amanuta Limitada
English translation copyright © 2025 Iris Enck
Translation arranged through MARINA Books Literary Agency, Barcelona, Spain

Copyright © Editorial Amanuta Limitada, Chile, 2022

10 9 8 7 6 5 4 3 2 1

0625 002

ISBN 978-1-83627-030-0

This book was typeset in Filson Pro, Fela and Tomarik.

Printed and manufactured in China by Leo Paper Products, Heshan,
Guangdong. June 2025.

This book conforms to General Product Safety Regulation (GPSR) requirements.

EU authorised representative: Harriet Birkinshaw, Post Wave Berlin Studio
Email: GPSR@postwavepublishing.com
Address: Post Wave Berlin Studio, c/o Mindspace, Skalitzer Straße 104, 10997
Berlin, Germany

REPTILES AND AMPHIBIANS

Nature's Most Extraordinary Creatures

Marty Crump and Andy Charrier

Illustrated by Loreto Salinas

Translated by Iris Enck

post wave

CONTENTS

4   INTRODUCTION

6   ORIGINS

8   EVOLUTIONARY TREE

10   WHAT IS AN AMPHIBIAN?

14   WHAT IS A REPTILE?

18   IMPORTANCE

20   SKIN

24   TEMPERATURE

26   SENSES

30   DIET

34   COMMUNICATION

36   REPRODUCTION AND LIFE CYCLE

40   DEFENCE AND ADAPTATION

44   CONSERVATION

46   FURTHER READING AND RESOURCES

47   GLOSSARY

49   BIBLIOGRAPHY

Green anaconda
Eunectes murinus

INTRODUCTION

Amphibians and reptiles are some of the Earth's most incredible creatures: there are thousands of species in many different colours, shapes and sizes. They can adapt easily, have a variety of defence mechanisms and so much more. They are ectotherms, which means they depend on external sources for their body heat, so their temperature changes with the environment.

But the most impressive thing about them is that they have existed for millions of years, and were the first living things to emerge from the water and to colonise and inhabit land.

You will learn many things in this book, including what types of amphibians and reptiles exist, how they have adapted, how they survive, their 'superpowers' – such as changing colour, seeing temperature and camouflaging themselves – their survival strategies, how they find mates and much more. By getting to know these animals, we gain insight into the mysteries of evolution, adaptation and the incredible diversity of life on our planet.

Herpetologists are scientists who study amphibians and reptiles. They teach us about these beautiful, multifaceted and mysterious creatures.

ORIGINS

Amphibians and reptiles are tetrapods, just like birds and mammals. Tetrapods were the first four-legged vertebrate to colonise the Earth. They lived in water but gradually moved onto dry land to eat, find new places to live, lay their eggs and escape predators. Their emergence from water was one of the most important evolutionary events in history.

When tetrapods left their aquatic life, their skeletons and organs began to change. Without the buoyancy of water to support them, they needed stronger bones and muscles to bear their weight and move efficiently on land. So, across millions of years of evolution, their fins transformed into legs to be able to walk. Their respiratory system also changed from gills (which let them breathe underwater) to lungs, to breathe air. This adaptation was one of the most fantastic events in evolution and it has allowed them to continue living to this day.

Birds are closely related to crocodiles and are now considered reptiles. In this book, however, we will only look at animals traditionally considered reptiles: turtles, lizards, snakes, crocodiles and tuatara.

TETRAPODS

Tetrapods are four-legged vertebrate animals that existed 365 million years ago (during the Devonian period). They lay two types of eggs depending on their group.

LISSAMPHIBIA

Amphibians lay eggs with a soft mucous membrane.

AMNIOTE

Reptiles, birds and some mammals lay eggs with a hard outer shell containing three membranes.

AMPHIBIANS

REPTILES

Reptile embryos develop within their eggs, which are protected by a hard outer shell, allowing the eggs to be laid on land. In contrast, amphibian eggs do not have this protection and must be laid in aquatic environments to survive. This is why amphibians need water, or return to water sources, to reproduce, while reptiles do not. Learn more on page 36.

365 312 279

Carboniferous (359–299 million years ago)

Permian (299–252 million years ago)

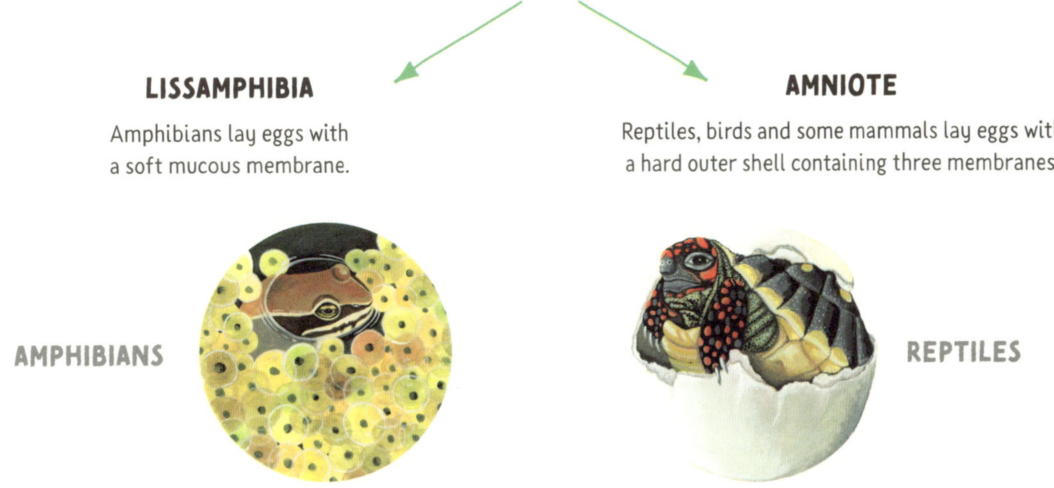

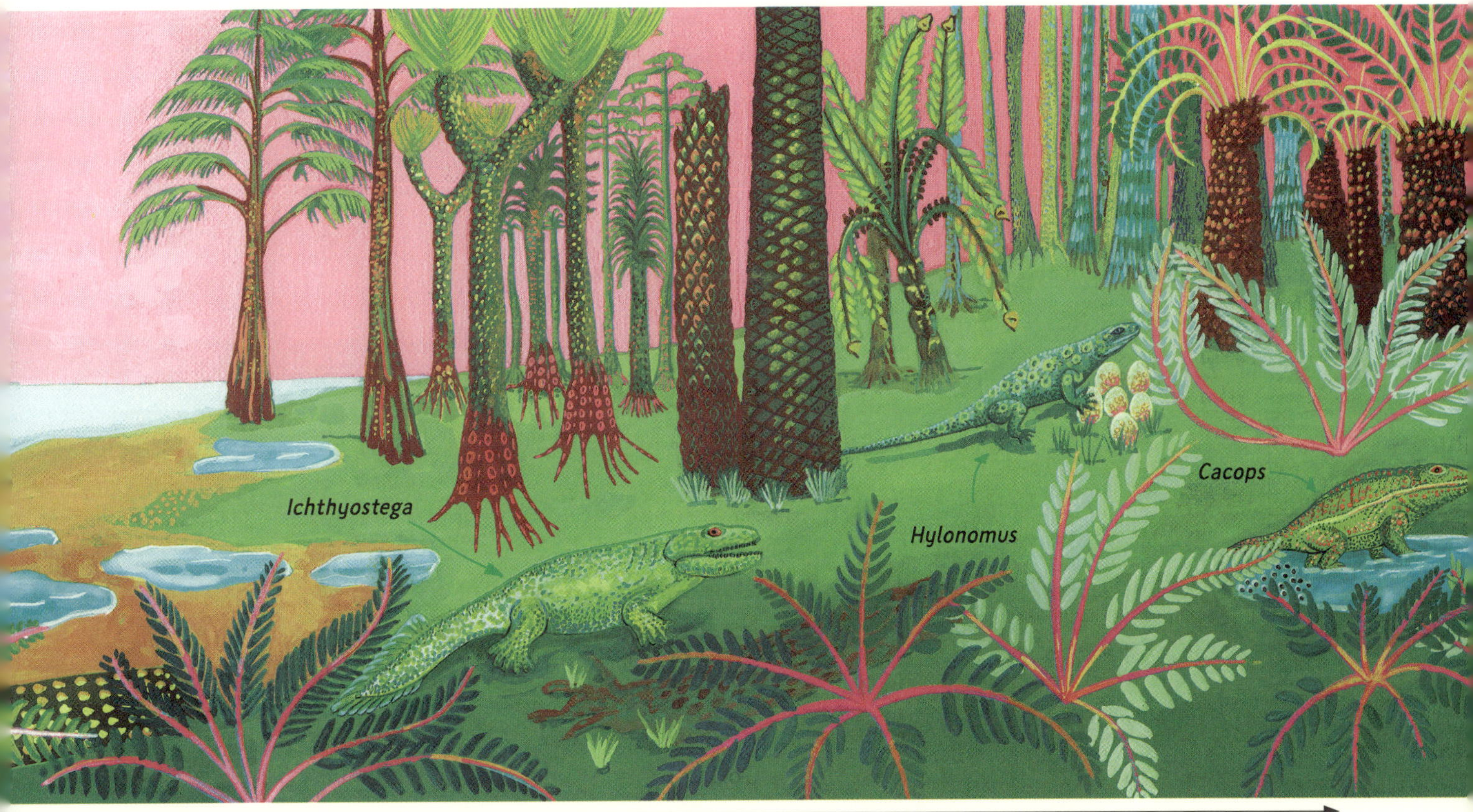

EVOLUTIONARY TREE

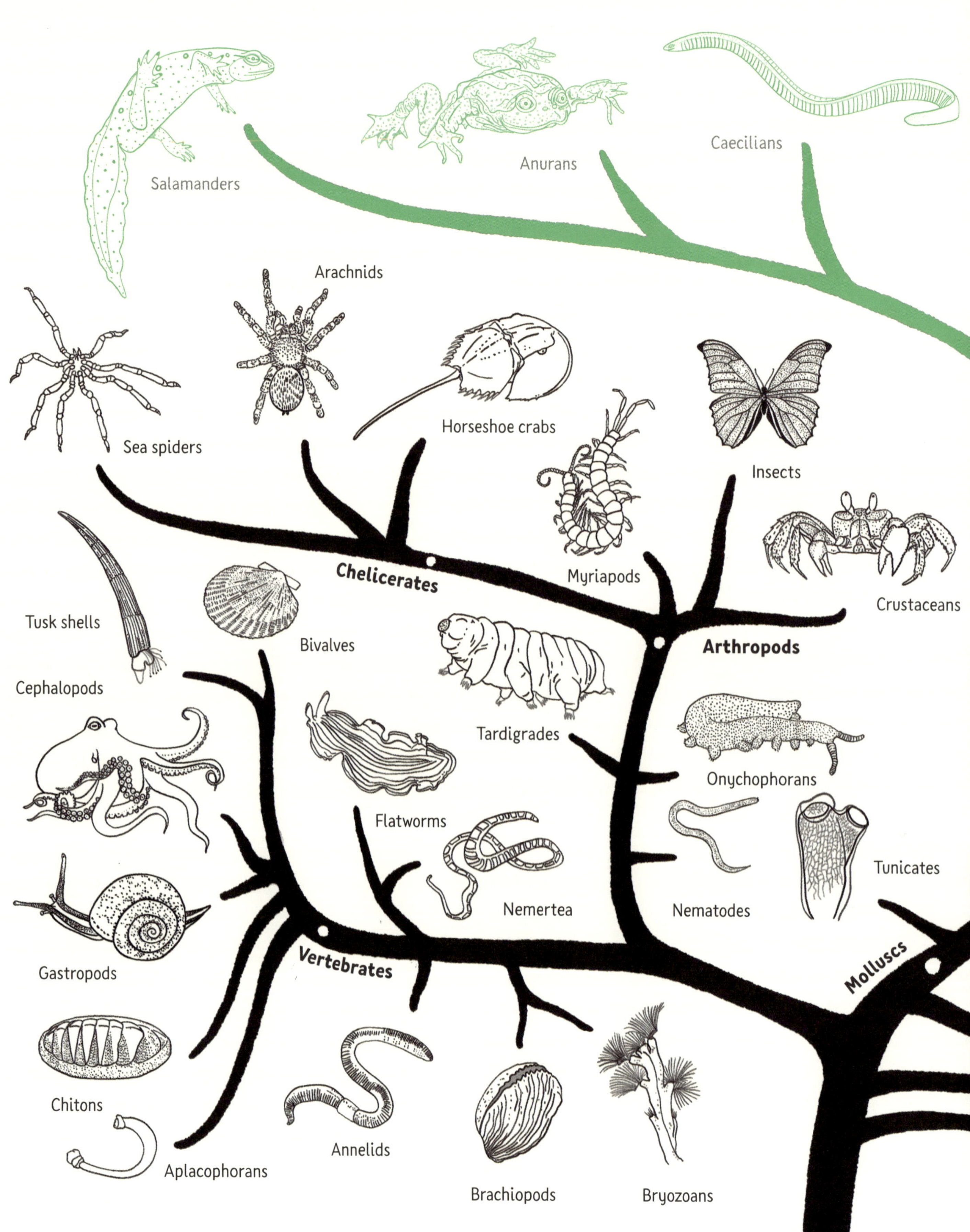

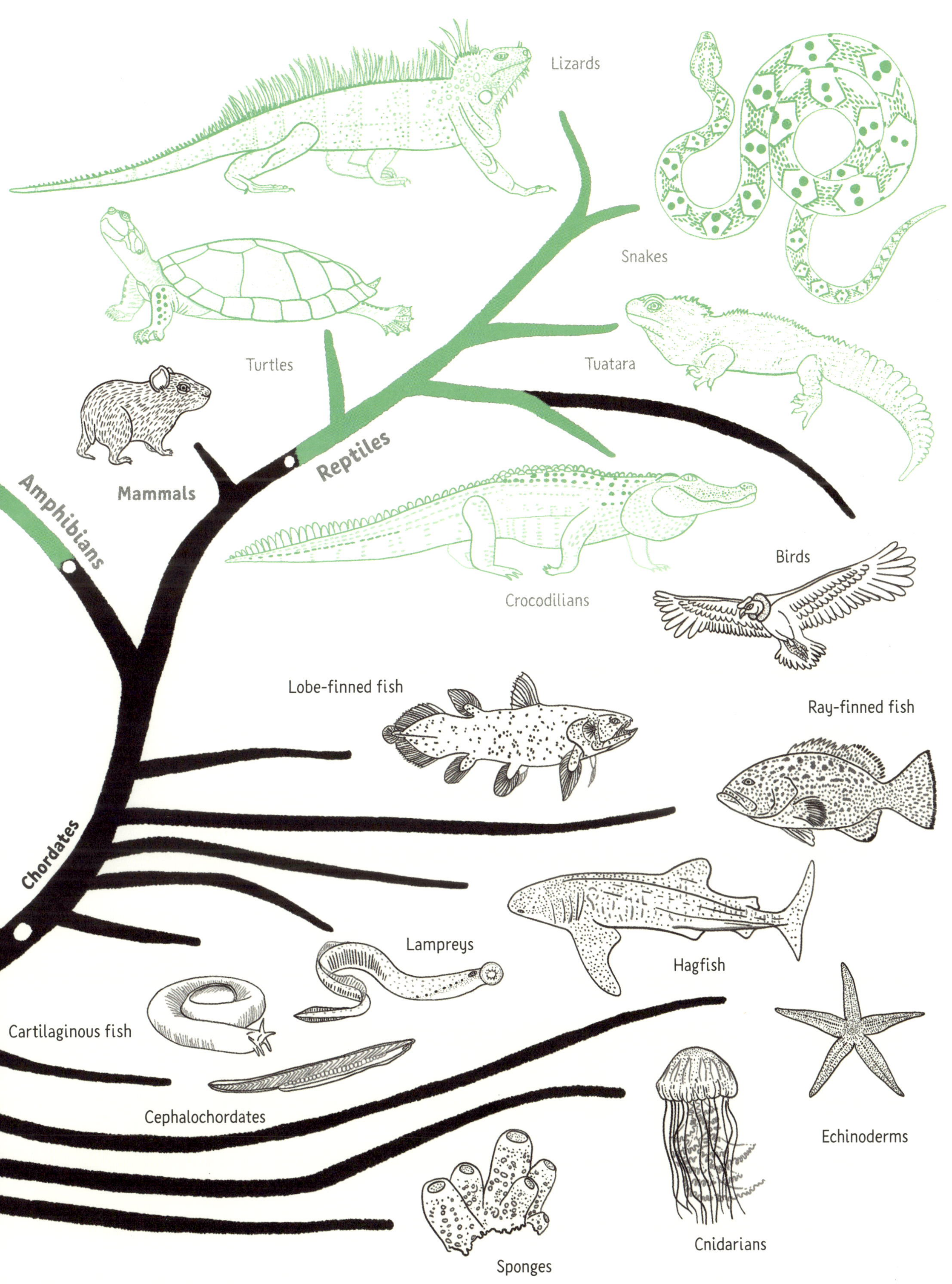

Lizards
Snakes
Turtles
Tuatara
Mammals
Reptiles
Amphibians
Birds
Crocodilians
Lobe-finned fish
Ray-finned fish
Chordates
Lampreys
Hagfish
Cartilaginous fish
Echinoderms
Cephalochordates
Cnidarians
Sponges

WHAT IS AN AMPHIBIAN?

The word 'amphibian' comes from the Latin word *amphibius* and means 'double life' because these animals can live both on land and in water. Amphibian larvae are completely aquatic, and the adults can be aquatic, semi-aquatic or terrestrial. Their skin has no fur, feathers or scales, and is used for breathing by drawing oxygen from the air and water.

Amphibians can live in many places and have successfully adapted to incredibly different environments, from sub-polar grasslands to tropical rainforests and even the desert! But they always live near water. Some live in trees, others underground and others underwater. Most amphibians are oviparous (meaning they produce young by laying eggs) and many of them are nocturnal.

Amphibians are grouped into orders, which are scientific categories that help classify animals based on their features. The three orders of amphibians are frogs and toads (Anura), salamanders and newts (Caudata), and caecilians (Gymnophiona).

CLASSIFICATION

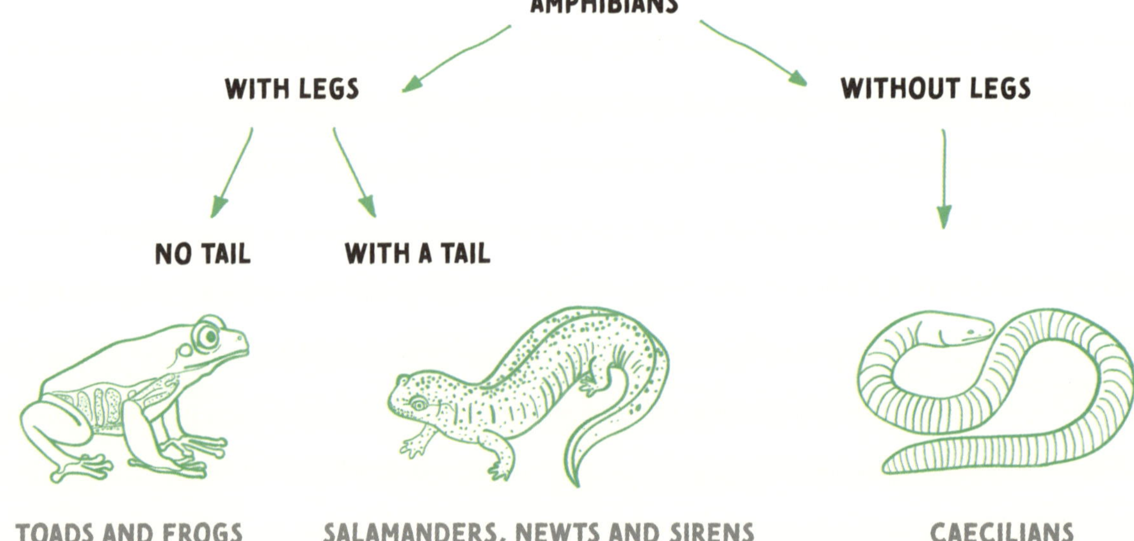

SEXUAL DIMORPHISM

For most amphibians, females can be identified at first glance thanks to their colouring and size, which is much larger than males.

Rio Pescado stubfoot toad
Atelopus balios

CAECILIANS (GYMNOPHIONA)

Caecilians are worm-like and live in tropical areas. Most species are blind, not requiring eyesight in their underground habitat, although some are aquatic. They are the most primitive group of amphibians and there are over 200 species, which is approximately three per cent of all amphibian species.

Caecilia tentaculata

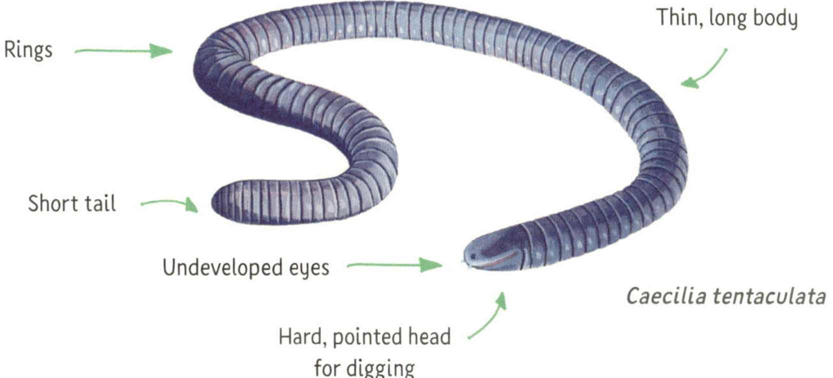

SALAMANDERS, NEWTS AND SIRENS (CAUDATA)

This group of amphibians all have legs and a tail. They include salamanders, newts and sirens. There are almost 750 species, making up nearly nine per cent of all amphibian species. The vast majority of them are aquatic or semi-aquatic, and salamanders are primarily found in warm environments.

SALAMANDER

Nimble long-limbed salamander
Nyctanolis pernix

NEWT

Eastern newt
Notophthalmus viridescens

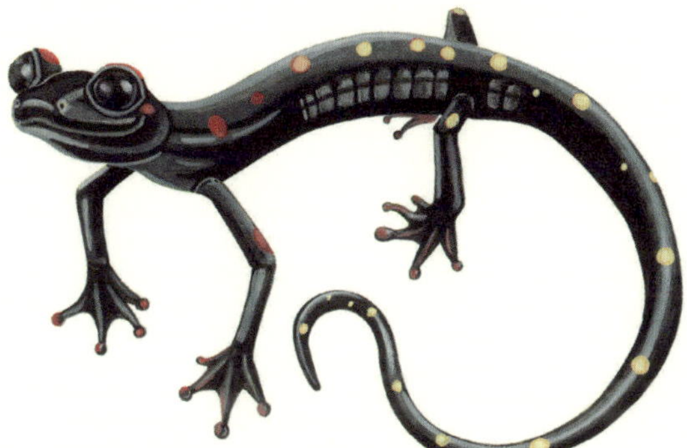

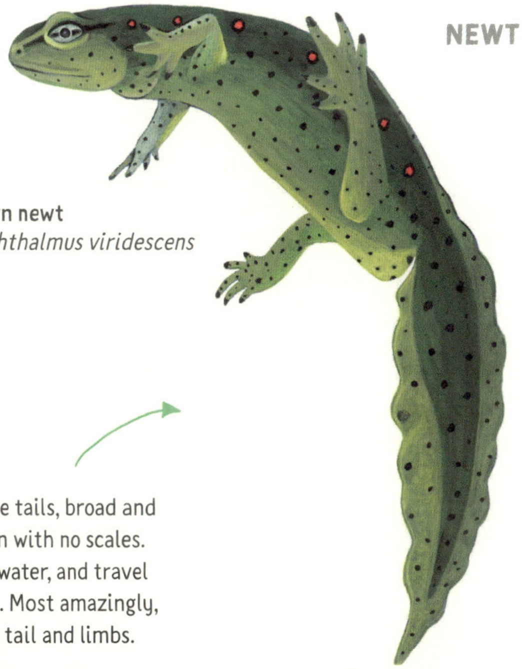

These amphibians have large tails, broad and flat heads, and smooth skin with no scales. They can live on land or in water, and travel with undulating movements. Most amazingly, they can regenerate their tail and limbs.

Large tail to propel themselves through water

SIREN

Greater siren
Siren lacertina

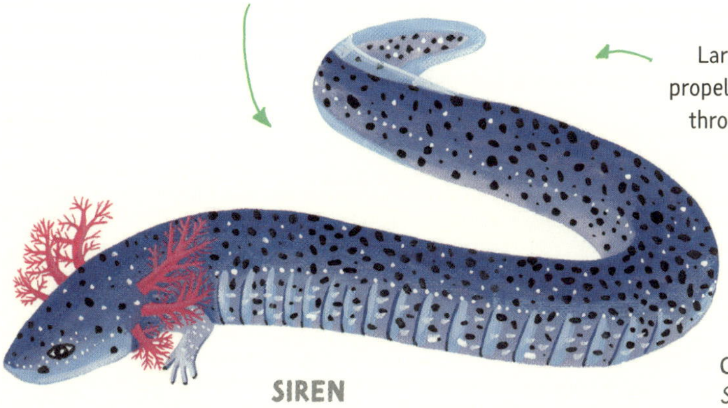

FROGS AND TOADS (ANURA)

This group of amphibians have strong hind legs that are more developed than their front legs, helping them jump. The name Anura literally means 'without a tail'. This group is the biggest and most diverse of all – around 88 per cent of amphibians are anurans and they are found all over the world. There are more than 7,000 species. Although many of us think that frogs and toads are the same, they have different characteristics.

ANATOMY OF FROGS AND TOADS

FROG

Slender body

Smooth, wet skin

Front legs with four fingers

Hind legs with five toes

Long legs and fingers

Emerald forest frog
Hylorina sylvatica

TOAD

Thick, muscular and round body

Dry, rough skin covered with glands

Short legs

Plains spadefoot toad
Spea bombifrons

PRETTY PUPILS

Amphibians have a diverse range of pupil shapes and colours. Look at all these beautiful eyes!

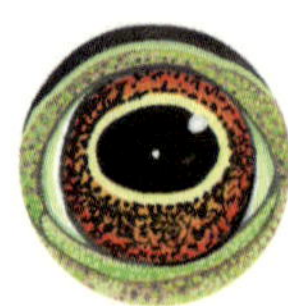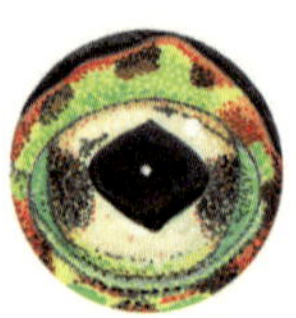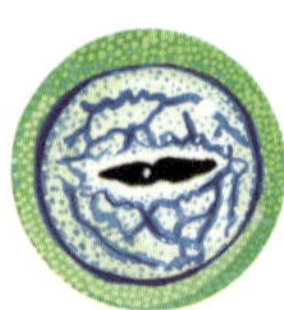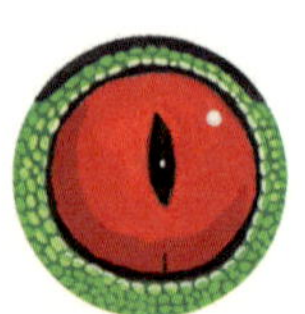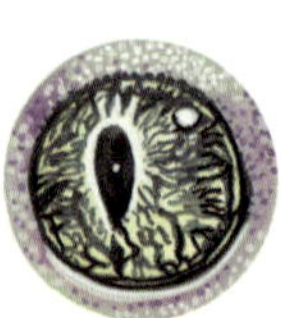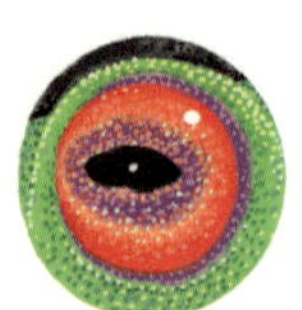

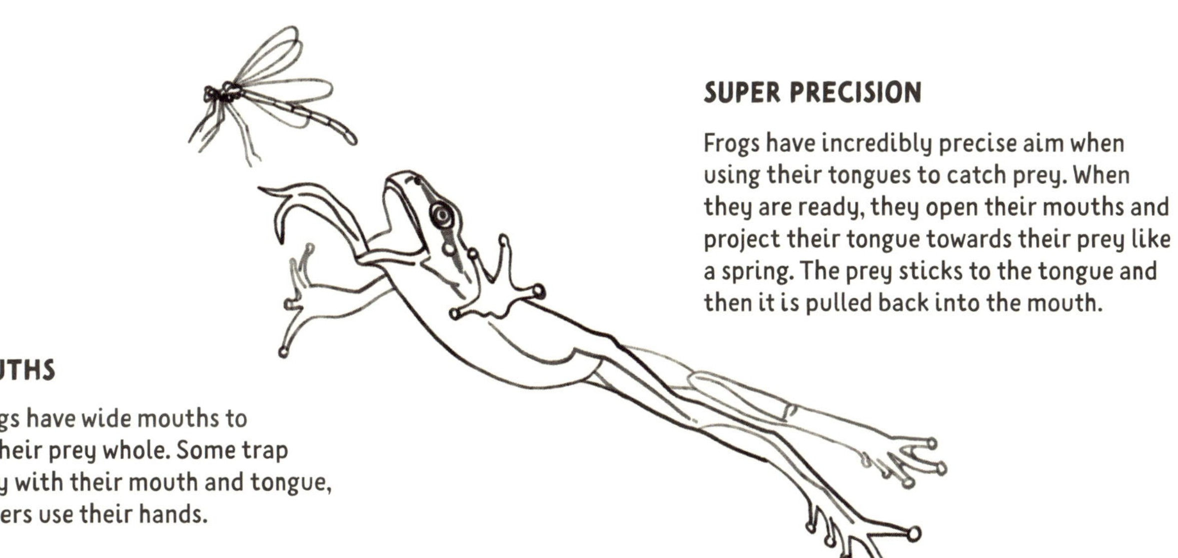

SUPER PRECISION

Frogs have incredibly precise aim when using their tongues to catch prey. When they are ready, they open their mouths and project their tongue towards their prey like a spring. The prey sticks to the tongue and then it is pulled back into the mouth.

BIG MOUTHS

Many frogs have wide mouths to swallow their prey whole. Some trap their prey with their mouth and tongue, while others use their hands.

FABULOUS FEET

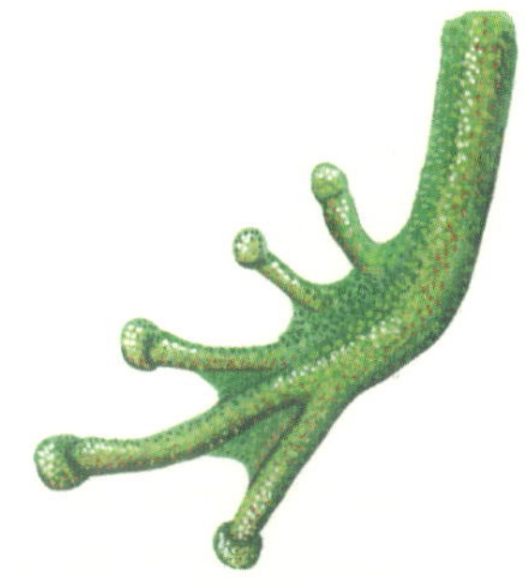

DIVING

Many frogs have webbed feet – membranes of skin between their fingers and toes, allowing them to swim as if they had diving fins. Frogs living in drier places tend to have less webbing or none at all.

EXCAVATING

Some frogs and toads have thick fingers and toes that help them migrate during severe droughts. And some use their front legs to dig and find refuge away from predators or the heat of summer.

CLIMBING

Some frogs have sticky pads on the tips of their fingers and toes to help them climb trees, branches and leaves. Thanks to these sticky pads, the frogs can also hang upside down.

Tiger-striped tree frog
Callimedusa tomopterna

ACROBATIC JUMPS

Most frog legs have special elastic tendons, allowing them to jump incredibly high for their size.

WHAT IS A REPTILE?

The word 'reptile' comes from the Latin word *reptilis*, meaning 'an animal that crawls'. Today, there are more than 10,800 recognised species of reptile. This number changes as some species become extinct while others are discovered. Reptiles all breathe through their lungs and have dry skin that is covered in scales. Most of them lay eggs, but turtles and snakes are viviparous, meaning the young develop inside the parent's body before being born.

The four main orders of reptiles are crocodiles and alligators (Crocodilia), lizards and snakes (Squamata), turtles and tortoises (Testudines) and tuataras (Rhynchocephalia).

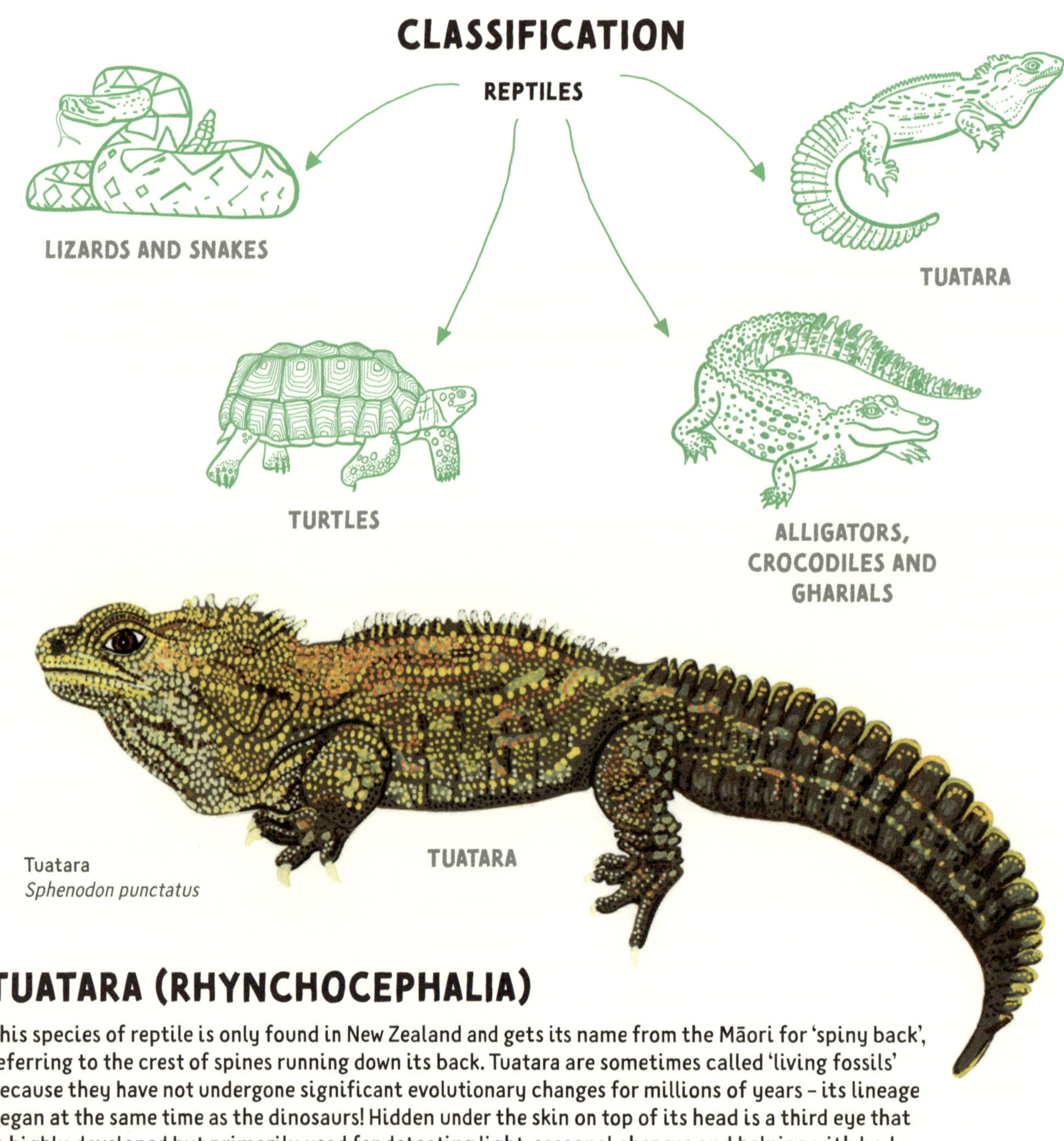

Tuatara
Sphenodon punctatus

TUATARA (RHYNCHOCEPHALIA)

This species of reptile is only found in New Zealand and gets its name from the Māori for 'spiny back', referring to the crest of spines running down its back. Tuatara are sometimes called 'living fossils' because they have not undergone significant evolutionary changes for millions of years – its lineage began at the same time as the dinosaurs! Hidden under the skin on top of its head is a third eye that is highly developed but primarily used for detecting light, seasonal changes and helping with body temperature regulation.

LIZARDS AND SNAKES (SQUAMATA)

Squamata are the most abundant reptiles, making up 96 per cent of them. We currently know of around 7,000 lizard and 4,000 snake species. They live in many different places like underground in soil or high up in trees, and across the world from deserts to rainforests – except for Antarctica. There are some similarities between lizards and snakes, but also some important differences. For example, both can shed their skin, but most lizards have legs and eyelids while snakes do not.

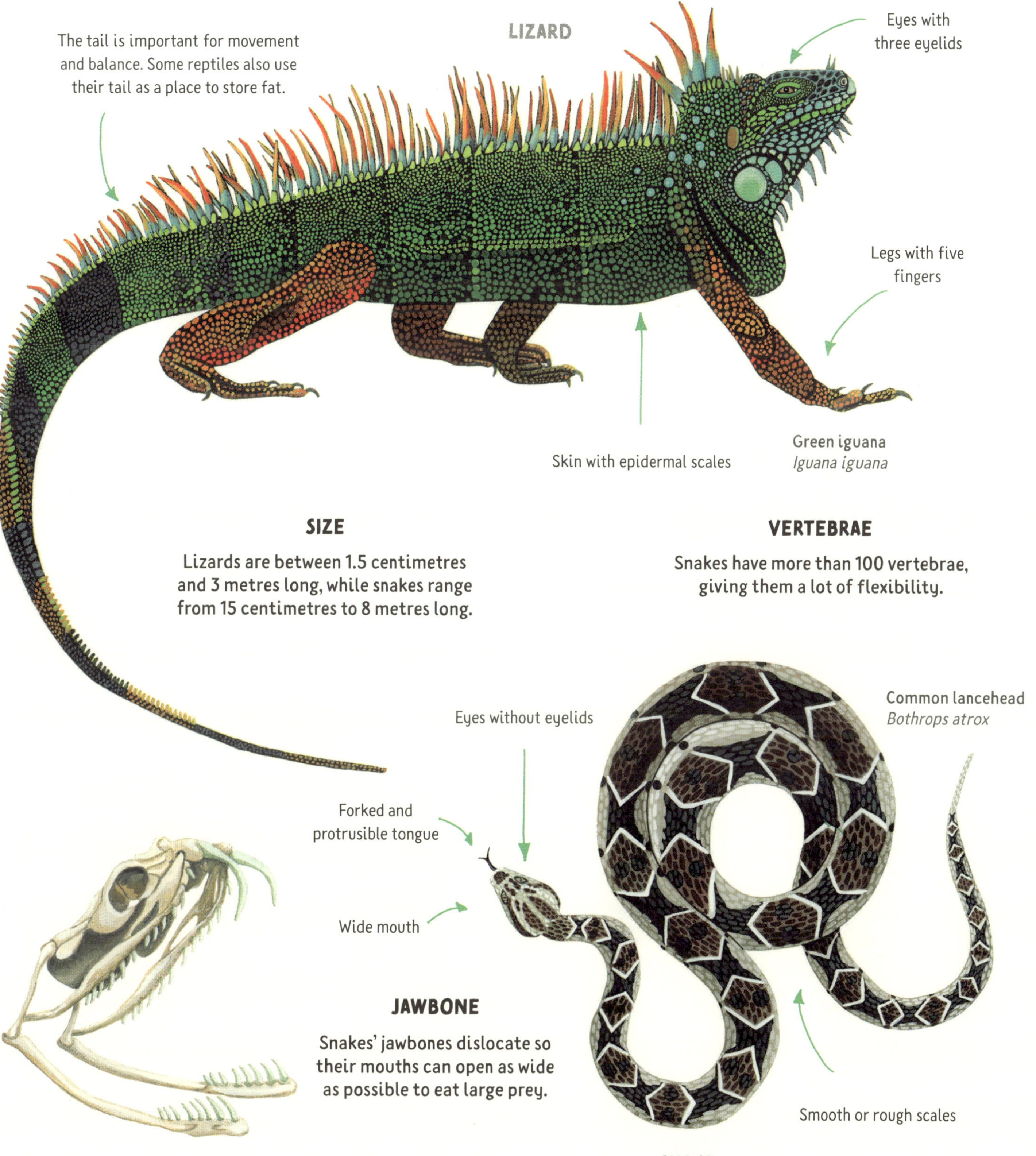

SIZE

Lizards are between 1.5 centimetres and 3 metres long, while snakes range from 15 centimetres to 8 metres long.

VERTEBRAE

Snakes have more than 100 vertebrae, giving them a lot of flexibility.

JAWBONE

Snakes' jawbones dislocate so their mouths can open as wide as possible to eat large prey.

TURTLES (TESTUDINES)

Turtles have existed for more than 240 million years and make up three per cent of all reptiles. Currently, there are more than 350 turtle species. Their bodies are covered by shells to protect them from predators. There are land turtles (commonly called tortoises) and aquatic turtles that live in salt water or fresh water.

SEA TURTLE

TORTOISE

FRESHWATER TURTLE

Arrau turtle
Podocnemis expansa

JAWS

Turtles don't have teeth. Instead, they have strong, sharp jaws for cutting and crushing, which are similar to the beaks of birds.

TURTLE LEGS

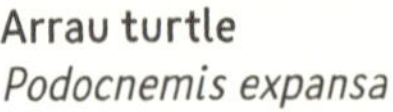

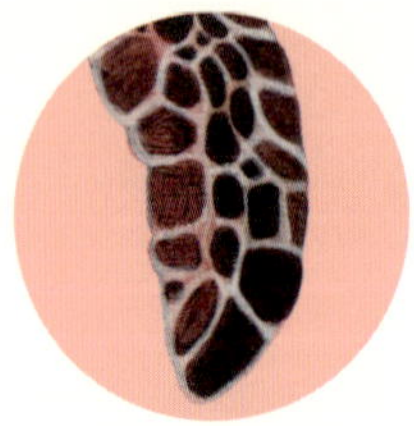

FIN-SHAPED

Found on sea turtles and are used to swim and dive.

WEBBED

Freshwater turtles use these to swim and walk.

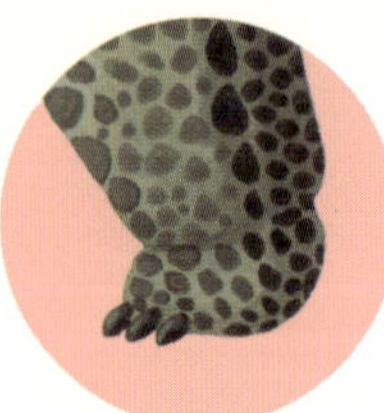

TUBULAR

Tortoises use their legs to walk.

SHELL

The carapace, which is the upper section of the shell, protects vital organs and is made of bone and skin. The bottom part of the shell is called the plastron. There are hard-shell turtles and softshell turtles.

ALLIGATORS, CROCODILES AND GHARIALS (CROCODILIA)

The order Crocodilia makes up less than one per cent of all reptiles. They are very big, and have scales and bony plates, so their skin is thicker than that of snakes and lizards. This gives them excellent protection. They are semi-aquatic, live only in tropical and subtropical zones, and spend most of their time submerged in water. They are capable of attacking almost any animal that enters their territory, but are also one of the most affectionate reptiles with their young.

CROCODILE

Crocodiles have the most powerful jaws in the animal kingdom.

Orinoco crocodile
Crocodylus intermedius

Crocodiles propel themselves through the water with their long, powerful tail. They also use it as a weapon, knocking prey or potential threats into the water.

Although their legs are short, they can run short distances very quickly. Usually, they move by crawling slowly.

Their teeth fall out and are replaced continuously throughout their life, which can happen up to 50 times.

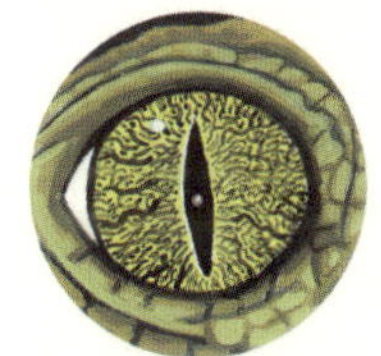

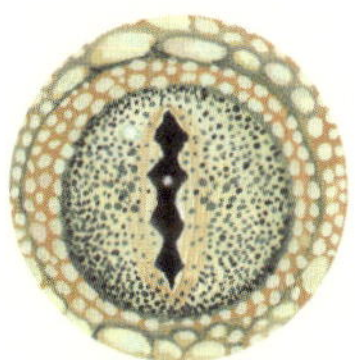

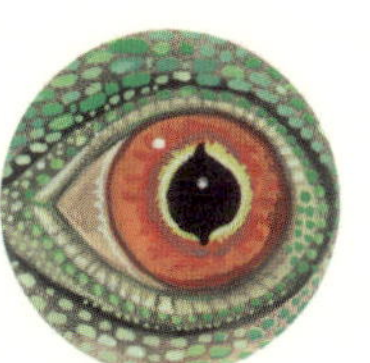

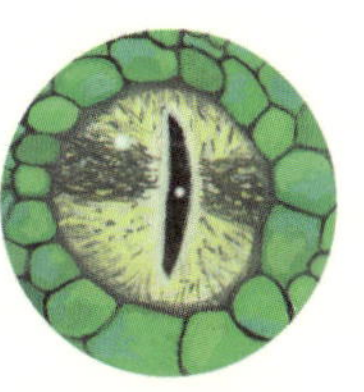

DISTINCT PUPILS

Reptile pupils vary according to lifestyle, habitat and species.

Caiman

Gecko

Iguana

Snake

DIFFERENCES BETWEEN CROCODILES AND ALLIGATORS

CROCODILE

Snout is thin and pointed, making a 'V' shape

Bigger in size

Live in both fresh and saltwater

Upper and lower teeth are visible when mouth closed

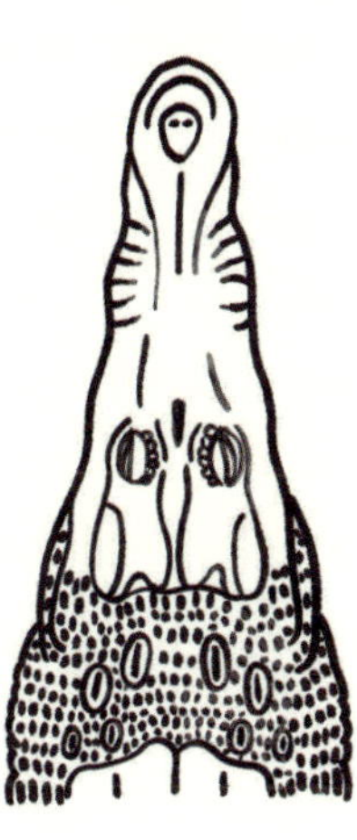

ALLIGATOR

Snout is wide and round, making a 'U' shape

Smaller in size

Live in fresh water only

Only the upper teeth are visible when mouth closed

IMPORTANCE

Amphibians and reptiles play an important role in an ecosystem, which is a community of living things, like animals and plants, interacting with each other and their environment. Every living thing helps to keep nature balanced in different ways.

Amphibians and reptiles are vital to the food chain, acting as both predators and prey.

They play a crucial role in the cycle of energy and nutrient exchange between the aquatic and terrestrial ecosystem.

They disperse seeds through their faeces.

Tadpoles that feed on algae keep the water clean (they prevent oxygen depletion caused by excessive algae overgrowth).

When turtles dig burrows in search of shelter, they unknowingly provide homes for many other animals, like insects, spiders, frogs and toads, lizards, snakes and small rodents.

Green sea turtles feed on algae and sea grass, which are crucial to the ocean's health – both provide oxygen and are home to many animals. Green sea turtles eat the tip of the sea grass (like a person mowing a lawn), which keeps it healthy. For this reason, green sea turtles are sometimes called 'gardeners of the sea'.

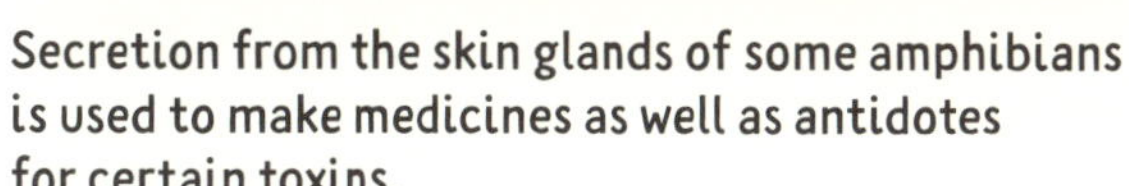

Secretion from the skin glands of some amphibians is used to make medicines as well as antidotes for certain toxins.

Scientists call some amphibians 'sentinels' because they act as warning signs of pollution in the environment.

SKIN

Skin allows living things to adapt to different habitats because it acts as a barrier against the environment they live in. Amphibians and reptiles have special skin that is more than just protection: it's a sensory organ important for their survival. It helps them maintain their body temperature, is vital for reproduction and they can communicate through their skin's colour and scent.

This tropical climbing salamander breathes through its skin.

Bolitoglossa peruviana

Lake Titicaca frog
Telmatobius culeus

BARE SKINNED

Amphibians are bare skinned, which means they do not have fur, feathers or scales. The skin is semipermeable, so they can breathe through it.

WRINKLY SKIN

The Lake Titicaca frog has lots of skin folds, allowing it to absorb more oxygen from the water in the high-altitude Altiplano plateau.

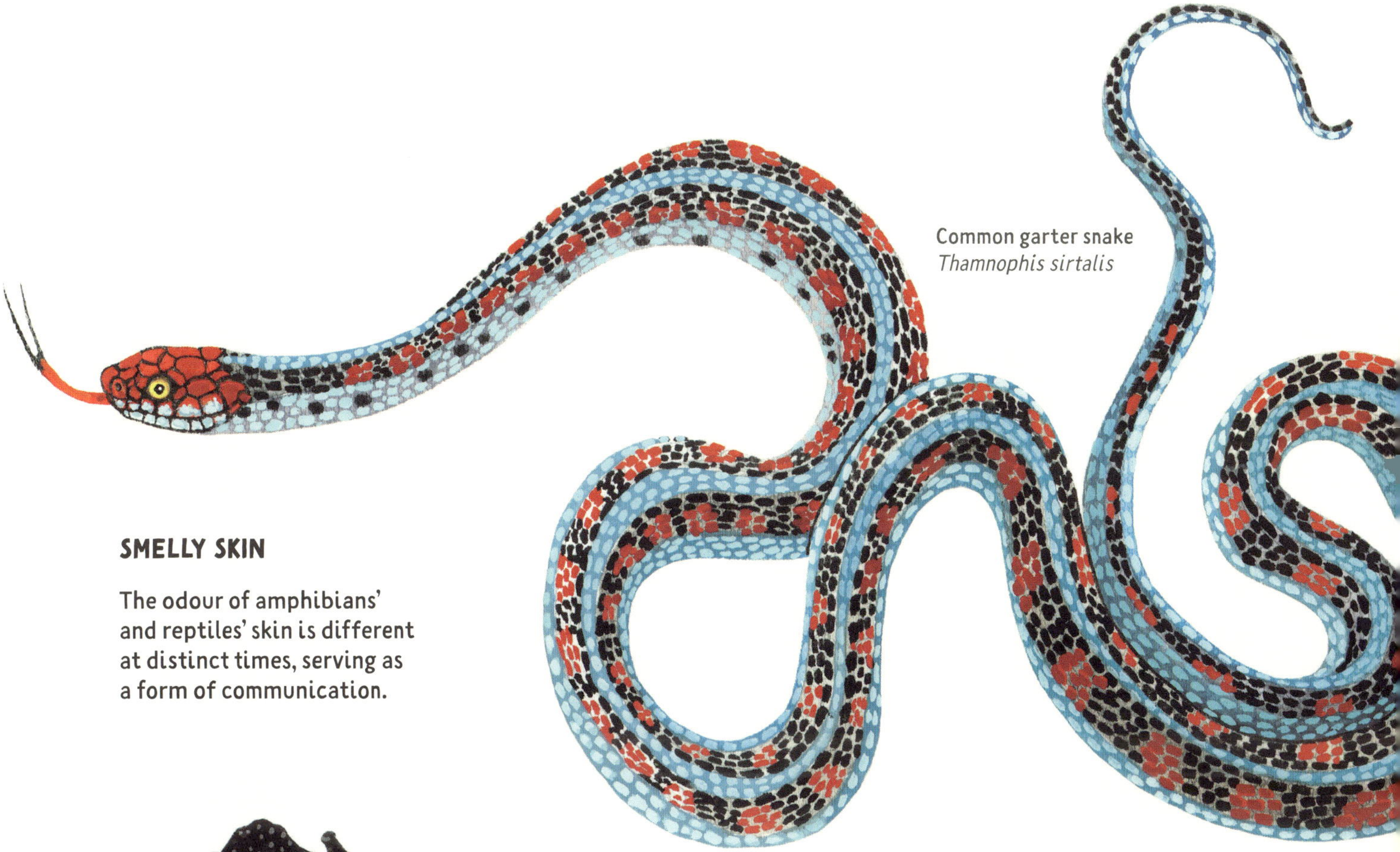

Common garter snake
Thamnophis sirtalis

SMELLY SKIN

The odour of amphibians'
and reptiles' skin is different
at distinct times, serving as
a form of communication.

SENSITIVE SKIN

Amphibian skin is very sensitive to the humidity
and acidity of the environment, so it's important
that the skin avoids dehydration.

Roraima bush toad
Oreophrynella quelchii

TRANSPARENT SKIN

Glass frogs are mostly green in colour
but have translucent skin on their bellies,
allowing you to see their internal organs
and bones through their skin.

La Palma glass frog
*Hyalinobatrachium
valerioi*

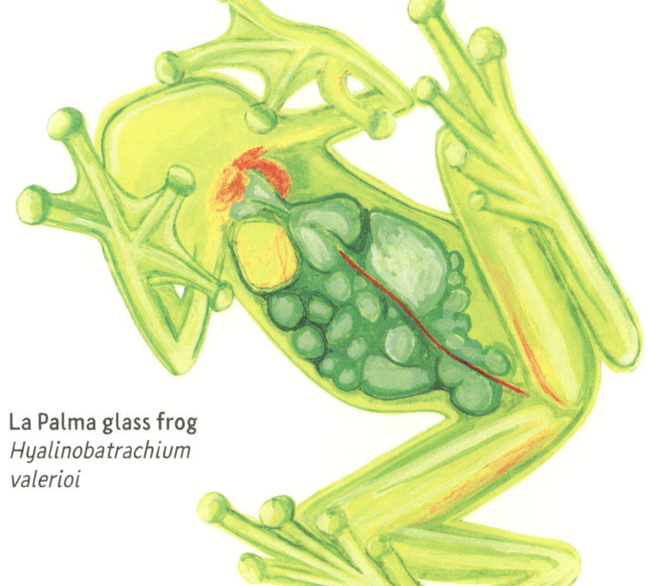

SENSATIONAL SCALES

Reptiles have dry, scaly skin. Their scales are made
of keratin, just like bird feathers and our nails.

Crocodile

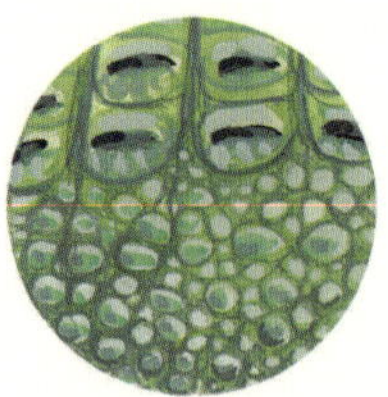

Lizard

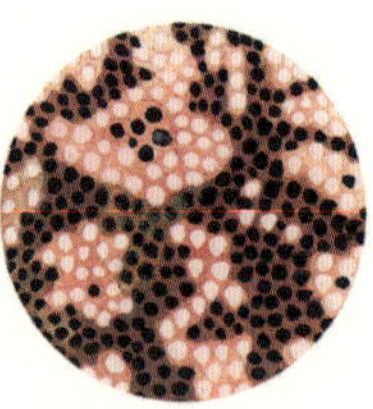

Snake

Turtle

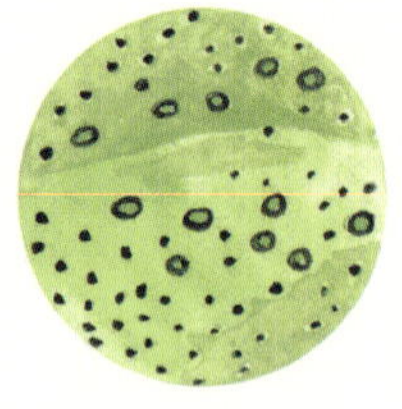

Crocodile scales
are strengthened
by bone plates.

Lizards have
various scales
with flexible
skin in between.

Snake scales
overlap each
other to give
them greater
protection.

Hard-shell turtles
have large, tough
scales.

Softshell turtles
have shells that are
covered with thick,
leathery skin.

Eastern coral snake
Micrurus fulvius

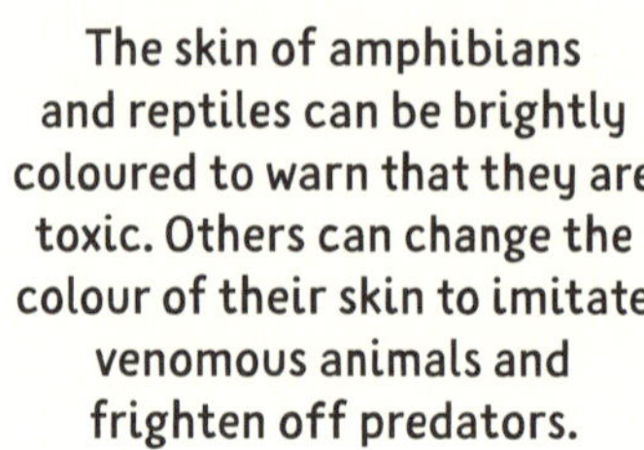

STRIKING COLOURS

The skin of amphibians
and reptiles can be brightly
coloured to warn that they are
toxic. Others can change the
colour of their skin to imitate
venomous animals and
frighten off predators.

LONG LIVE HUMIDITY!

Amphibians don't need to drink water because their
skin can absorb it. The downside is that they can
also dehydrate through their skin, which makes
them vulnerable to droughts, so for this reason,
most amphibians live in humid environments.

IN MINIATURE

The tiny Brazilian pygmy gecko
is only a couple of centimetres
long – about the size of a paperclip!
Its delicate toes easily stick to
leaves and other surfaces. It also
has hydrophobic skin, which means
it does not get wet – even raindrops
roll off quickly.

Brazilian pygmy gecko
Chatogekko amazonicus

SKIN SHEDDING

Reptiles change their skin throughout their life,
which is called moulting. This can be a complete
moult, which snakes do, where they shed a semi-
transparent layer from head to tail. Or it can be a
partial moult, where they either shed small, hardly
noticeable clumps of scales – the way turtles and
crocodiles do – or in large patches, like lizards.

Eastern coral snake
Micrurus fulvius

COUNTING MOULTS

Each time a rattlesnake
moults its skin, the rattle at
the tip of its tail gets longer.

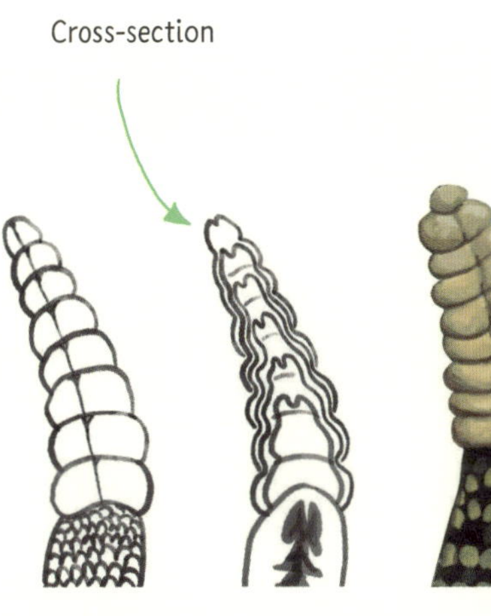

Argentine horned frog
Ceratophrys ornata

WARTS

Some toads are covered in warts.
But don't worry, they aren't contagious!
There are small warts that produce
toxic or unpleasant-tasting substances,
and there are large warts that contain
concentrated doses of toxins.

TEMPERATURE

Most living things need to keep their body temperature within a certain range to do daily activities such as move, look for shelter, eat, reproduce and sleep. They must take care that they don't freeze, and they must also prevent excess heat from affecting them.

ECTOTHERMS

Amphibians and reptiles cannot generate body heat on their own. They rely on the environment's temperature. To heat up, they need an external source like the sun.

Emerald swift
Sceleporus malachiticus

SUN WORSHIPPERS

When a lizard's body temperature drops, they orient their bodies at right angles towards the sun for maximum exposure to the sun's rays. They even seek out inclined surfaces to find the best angle.

Spotted false monitor
Callopistes maculatus

MALE OR FEMALE?

The sex of crocodiles, many tortoises and some lizards depends on the temperature at which the eggs are incubated. In some species, a male will hatch if the eggs are warmer. In other species, however, it will be a female.

COLD-BLOODED?

Some people use the term 'cold-blooded' to refer to amphibians and reptiles. But we now know that their blood is not actually cold. On a hot day, their blood is warm.

CHASING HEAT

Reptiles move from sunny areas to shady areas and vice versa, depending on the temperature they need at any given time. They bask in the sun or rest on warm surfaces. They need warmth to become active, forage for food and escape predators.

HUDDLE UP!

Some snakes are very sociable and like to spend the winter as a group to share their warmth with each other.

ANTI-FREEZE

Some amphibians, such as the wood frog, are able to lower their freezing point and create a layer of ice on their skin to tolerate extreme cold – an amazing survival skill! Other amphibians lighten the colour of their skin to absorb less heat.

Wood frog
Lithobates sylvaticus

American bullfrog
Lithobates catesbeianus

Mexican burrowing toad
Rhinophrynus dorsalis

COOLING OFF

Diurnal amphibians are active during the day and seek the sun's warmth, but sometimes the heat is too much. So, from time to time, they submerge themselves in water to regulate their temperature.

HOT MEALS

Amphibians hunt when their body temperature is high as they are most active in hot weather. When the temperature drops, they eat less. Some amphibians, like the Mexican burrowing toad, remain inactive during these periods, surviving solely on their reserves or other adaptive strategies.

SENSES

Sensory organs help amphibians and reptiles detect and understand their surroundings. There are five basic senses: sight, smell, touch, hearing and taste. Each group of amphibians or reptiles has a primary sense. Some can detect ultraviolet and infrared light, while others are able to detect the Earth's magnetic fields. These senses are of great importance when it comes to obtaining food, reproducing or protecting themselves from predators.

SIGHT

Emerald tree boa
Corallus caninus

SEEING HEAT

Reptiles are the only animals that can 'see' temperature and perceive the body heat of other living things. This helps them to know if there is another animal hidden nearby, to escape from predators and to hunt at night.

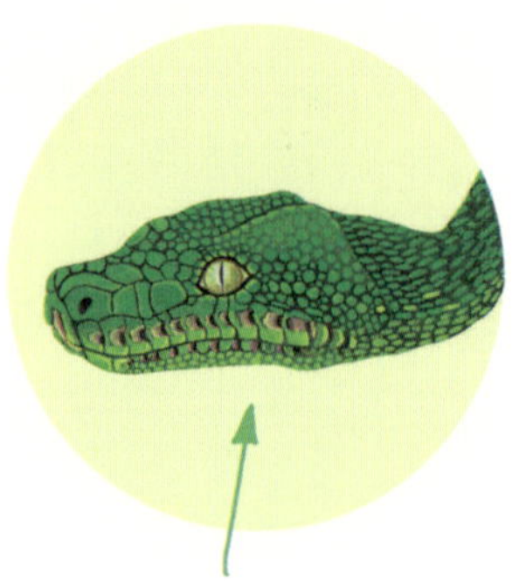

Pit organs are thermoreceptors that sit just below the eyes, and are able to detect heat emitted by another animal.

Cantillana spiny-chest frog
Alsodes cantillanensis

AMAZING EYES

Vision is very important for frogs. Some species have large, bulging eyes, which gives them 360-degree vision. Their eyes are located on top of their head, so they can still see while the rest of their body is hidden underwater.

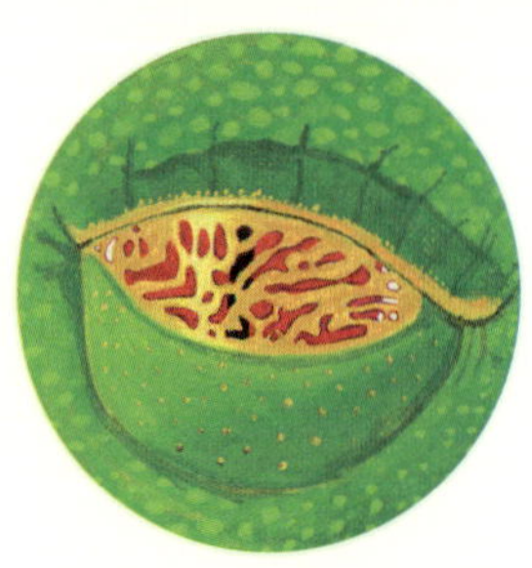

THIRD EYELID

Many reptiles and amphibians have a third eyelid, which is a transparent membrane that protects the eye, moistens it and allows them to see through it.

PINEAL EYE

The pineal eye, also called a third eye, is a photoreceptor organ under the animal's scales on top of their head. It helps to detect changes in light.

TASTE AND SMELL

SMELLING WITH THE TONGUE

When observing a lizard or snake, you may see its tongue flick in and out of its mouth. This movement is used to pick up chemicals from the air and ground, which the tongue carries to the vomeronasal organ on the roof of the mouth. Also known as Jacobson's organ, it is a sensitive structure that identifies odours and provides information about the environment.

Eastern hognose snake
Heterodon platirhinos

Hellbender salamander
Cryptobranchus alleganiensis

UNIQUE WAYS TO SMELL

Some amphibians use their excellent sense of smell to hunt, like the hellbender salamander. Others use the tentacles on the sides of their head as a nose to sniff, like the *Caecilia tentaculata*.

SMELLING UNDERWATER

A turtle's sense of smell is just as good underwater as it is on land.

Spiny softshell turtle
Apalone spinifera

GOOD TASTE

Crocodiles and alligators have an excellent sense of taste. They can tell if their food has gone bad, and if it has, will let it fall from their jaws.

Black caiman
Melanosuchus niger

TOUCH

SENSITIVE SKIN

Amphibians sense pain and temperature changes through their sense of touch. This helps them respond quickly to any external change.

FEELING EVERYTHING

The cave-dwelling Texas blind salamander has very small, non-functioning eyes. It senses everything through touch, which it even uses to find and court a mate.

FINGER FOOD

The common Surinam toad relies on touch to find its food. Its fingertips have suction lobes, which it uses to hunt since it has no tongue and only very small eyes.

Common Surinam toad
Pipa pipa

Texas blind salamander
Eurycea rathbuni

Salamanders
in courtship

THICK SKIN

Amphibians and reptiles are very sensitive to touch all over their bodies. But the more scales they have, the less sensitive they become. They are also less sensitive if they have a shell.

Red-footed tortoise
Chelonoidis carbonaria

HEARING

UNDERWATER SOUND

Amphibians and reptiles, with the exception of snakes, can hear sounds whether they are above or below water.

Green sea turtle
Chelonia mydas

BORN TALKING

When crocodiles hatch, they quickly start emitting sounds to communicate with each other.

GOOD VIBRATIONS

Snakes don't have external hearing, so they cannot hear or feel vibrations in the air like other reptiles. Instead, they rest their jaw on the ground to feel vibrations, and use this to locate prey.

Red-eyed tree frog
Agalychnis callidryas

DIFFERENT EARDRUMS

Some amphibians have exposed eardrums, while others' eardrums are covered by skin.

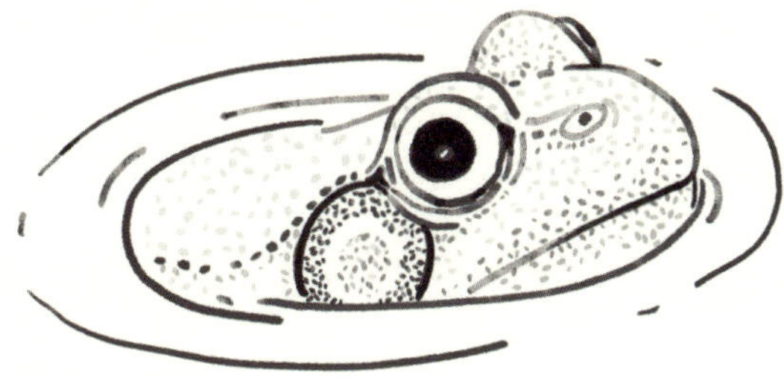

FROG EARS

Hearing is vital for survival. It allows frogs to escape from strange or dangerous noises, but also to communicate socially and mate. Female frogs will choose the males that sing best to be their mate.

DIET

Eating is necessary for any animal's survival, and there are as many types of food as there are species. Each species has different preferences and ways of getting its food. Most reptiles are carnivores, but many turtles are herbivores. Amphibians don't eat a wide variety of foods. Their larvae eat plants, but most adults switch to eating insects.

TASTY DIRT

When the green iguana hatches, it eats the soil in its nest, which contains bacteria that helps with digestion.

Catesby's snail-eater
Dipsas catesbyi

ELEGANT EATER

The Catesby's snail-eater has special fangs to remove snails from their shells and eat them.

HUNGRY SWIMMERS

The marine iguana swims to the bottom of the sea to eat nutritious algae, while sea turtles take advantage of the ocean's currents to search for their food.

Marine iguana
Amblyrhynchus cristatus

BITE-SIZED SNACKS

Amphibians eat insects, spiders and some invertebrates like slugs and worms. But larger amphibians can hunt small mammals – the American bullfrog can eat mice and even other frogs.

American bullfrog
Lithobates catesbeianus

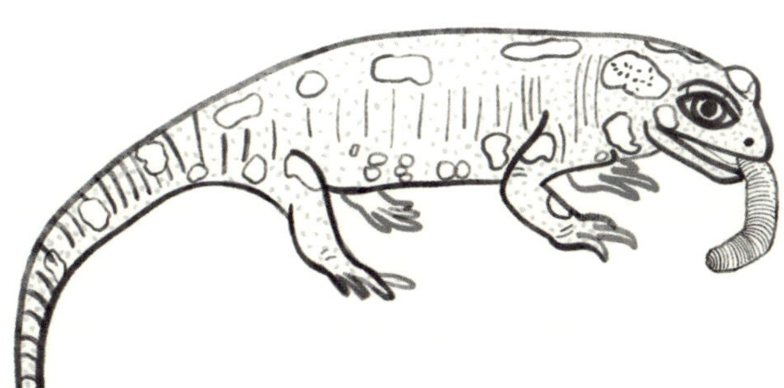

NOT FUSSY

Amphibians are opportunists and eat whatever they find in their habitat. Since they do not travel in search of food, their diet is less varied. There are aquatic amphibians whose diets consist of only fish and larvae.

SNEAKY TRICKS

The alligator snapping turtle has a worm-shaped appendage on its tongue, which it uses to attract prey.

STRONG JAWS

Turtles lack teeth but have powerful jaws to cut and crush food. Aquatic turtles, which are carnivorous, have a much stronger bite than land turtles, which are herbivorous.

Alligator snapping turtle
Macrochelys temminckii

HUNTING STYLES

Carnivorous reptiles have different ways of getting their food. Some stalk and ambush their prey, others run and chase them and some set traps and trick them.

SNIPERS

Some amphibians are hunters. They have an agile body, a sticky tongue and small teeth, which are all assets when it comes to catching prey.

Mata mata
Chelus fimbriatus

SUCKED IN

The mata mata is a type of turtle that sits on the ocean floor, patiently waiting for its next meal. When a fish gets close, it opens its mouth and throat, generating a strong suction current that pulls the prey into its mouth.

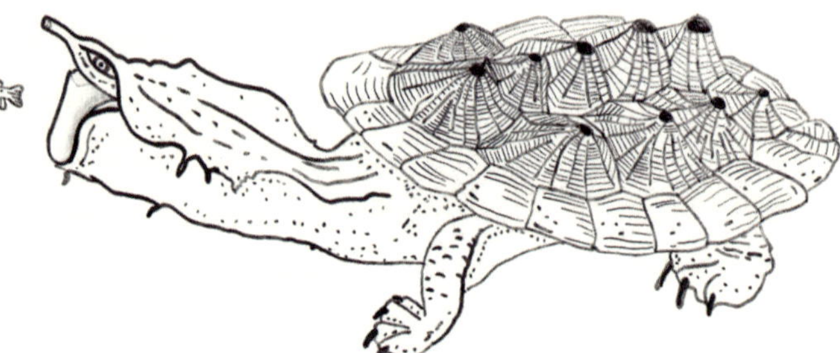

Green anaconda
Eunectes murinus

SNAKE SKILLS

Some snakes use their teeth to stop prey from escaping. Others inject venom to subdue them. Constrictors, such as boas and pythons, wrap around their prey and squeeze until the prey suffocates or their heart stops beating.

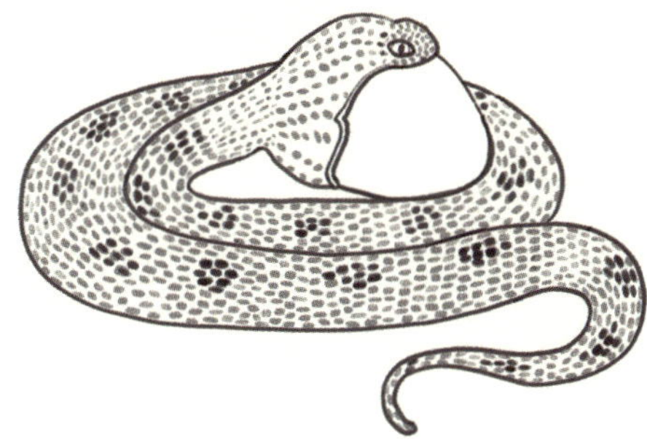

BIG BITES

Snakes can dislocate their jaw to swallow prey that is larger than their heads. Once the prey is partially inside the snake's mouth, it moves its jawbone from one side to the other until the animal falls into its throat.

Highland eyelash-pitviper
Bothriechis schlegelii

AMBUSH

The highland eyelash-pitviper hunts at night, hiding itself and waiting patiently for its prey.

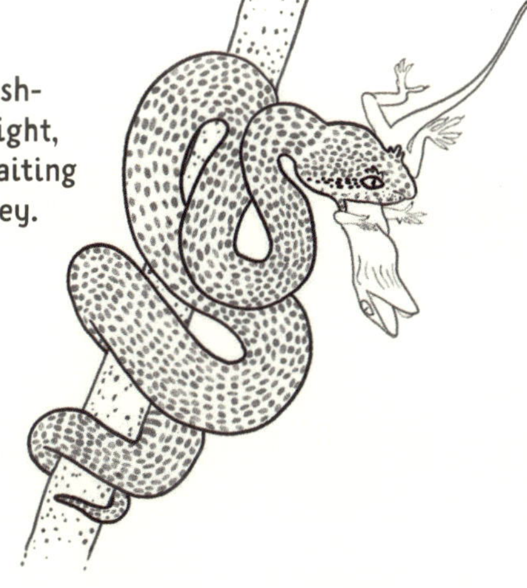

ELEMENT OF SURPRISE

The Argentine horned frog has an enormous mouth and bulging eyes. It sinks into the mud so only its eyes are visible. When its prey gets near, it jumps up and swallows it quickly.

Argentine horned frog
Ceratophrys ornata

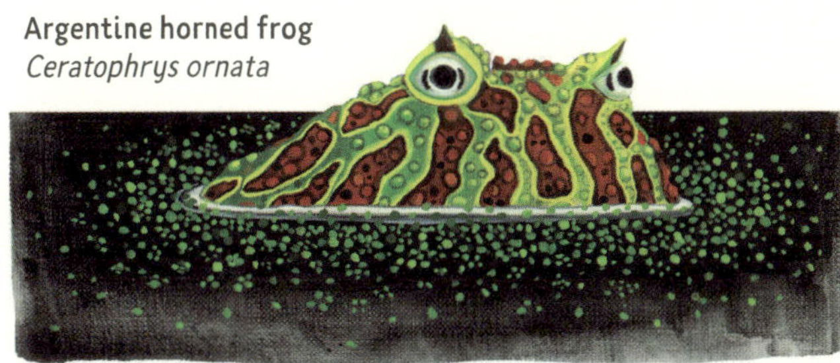

IN ONE BITE

Crocodile teeth are designed for gripping and cutting, not chewing. They crush their prey and then swallow it whole. Some species swallow stones to help break down their food.

COMMUNICATION

Communication plays an essential role in reproduction, feeding and defence. Calls help amphibians find mates and defend their territory. They also use smells and sights to share information about food or danger.

PHEROMONES

In the aquatic world, relying on sight and sound is not always enough. Amphibians can also detect different substances in the water, which helps them survive. These strong-smelling substances are called pheromones, which they can produce and recognise from other animals.

Panamanian golden frog
Atelopus zeteki

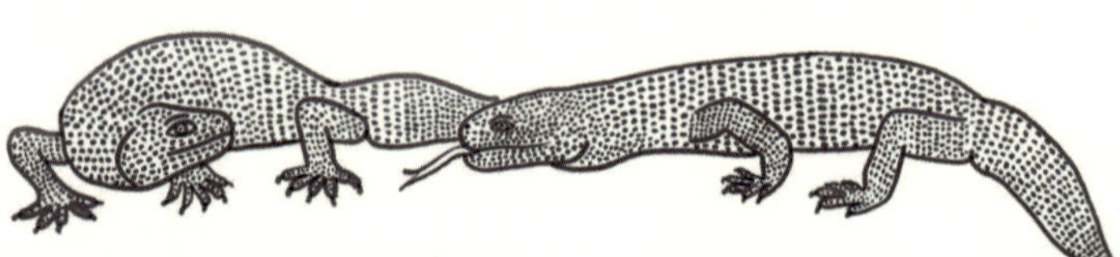

CHEMISTRY

Lizards determine if the other is male or female by receiving chemical information through their tongues.

INVISIBLE BORDERS

Some male lizards leave secretions on rocks and paths as they walk. This is how they mark their territory, which other lizards identify with their tongues.

American green tree frog
Dryophytes cinereus

LOVE SONGS

Frogs and toads sing to find a mate. Their calls travel quickly and can pass through trees, leaves and other noises, helping them hear each other even when they can't see. In general, males tend to sing more.

EXPRESSIVE TURTLES

Turtles mainly communicate with each other when they're looking for a mate or when they fight. They use their body language to communicate by moving their heads or opening their mouths as a threat. To differentiate between males and females, they use chemical and tactile signs. For example, the male may strike or rub the female's head with its claws.

American alligator
Alligator mississippiensis

SHOUTING MATCH

Male alligators scream out loud to announce their ownership of territories, to attract females and when they fight. Female alligators emit soft sounds to communicate with their young.

Green anole
Anolis carolinensis

LOTS OF COLOUR

Anole lizards can change their colour from brown to bright green, depending on their mood, stress levels, activity and interaction with other individuals.

DRAMATIC

Salamanders use their entire body to communicate. They display different poses to express themselves.

Red salamander
Pseudotriton ruber

SCENT OF LOVE

Snakes communicate with visual, tactic and chemical signals. When females are ready to mate, they produce chemical substances on their skin. Males are attracted to these chemicals. When they find a mate, the male may communicate through strokes, chin rubs, pushing against or even biting the female.

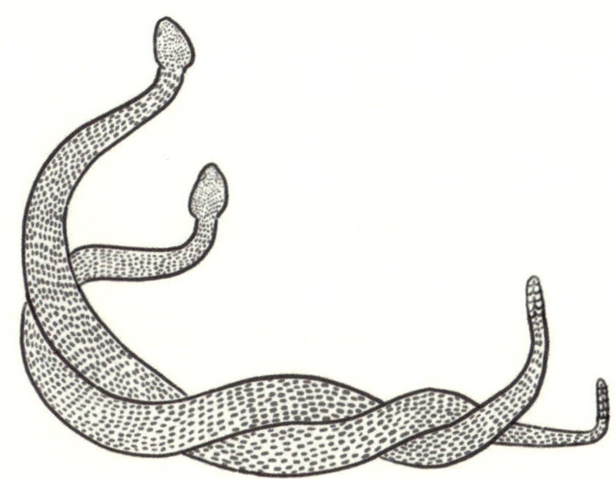

REPRODUCTION AND LIFE CYCLE

Living things continue to exist because they reproduce. Each animal has particular ways
of attracting a partner and knowing when and how they should approach the other. Some
only partner up to reproduce, some also raise their young together, and some stay together
forever. There are amphibians and reptiles that reproduce by laying eggs, while others are
viviparous and develop their young inside their bodies.

DISTINCT TYPES OF EGGS

Reptile eggs have a protective layer and membranes
that allow for the embryo's development, nutrition
and hydration. In contrast, amphibian eggs are soft,
without external protection, and they dry out easily.
Therefore, they are laid in humid places or in water.
Most reptiles lay individual eggs, while amphibians
lay eggs in chains or groups.

Frog egg

Alligator egg

LAYING EGGS

Turtles and crocodiles lay their eggs in
burrowed nests. Lizards and snakes leave
their eggs protected in a safe place.

MATING EMBRACE

With most amphibians, fertilisation occurs outside of the body,
in water. This is called amplexus – the male embraces the female,
and the male fertilises the eggs as they are released from the
female's body.

Golden toad
Incilius periglenes

Gills

Salamander larva

Egg

When they hatch from
their eggs, reptiles look
almost exactly the same
as they will look for the
rest of their lives.

American alligator
Alligator mississippiensis

All amphibian larvae
are aquatic, so they
have gills to breathe.

METAMORPHOSIS

Amphibians grow and change through a process called metamorphosis. A larva or tadpole starts life in water and later moves to land as an adult. At first, the tadpole has gills to breathe underwater, a round mouth to eat algae and decaying plants, and a tail for swimming. As it grows, legs and arms develop, and the tail slowly disappears.

NEOTENY

In some species of salamander, metamorphosis does not occur (or it is incomplete). This is called neoteny, meaning the amphibian reaches sexual maturity while still in the larval stage.

UNDER THE SKIN

The common Surinam toad lays its fertilised eggs on its back and covers them with skin. The eggs grow under the skin until they finish changing into froglets. Then, they break through the mother's skin and come out as tiny adult frogs.

The glass frog protects its eggs by camouflaging itself next to them.

UNUSUAL CARE

Darwin's frog lays up to 20 eggs in moss. The male attentively cares for them for about 20 days, until the eggs begin to move. Then, he swallows them and keeps them in his vocal sac, where they are kept safe until they fully develop.

Darwin's frog
Rhinoderma darwinii

Strawberry poison-dart frog
Oophaga pumilio

NUTRITIOUS FOOD

The strawberry poison-dart frog, also known as the blue jeans poison frog, lays its eggs in bromeliads – tropical plants that can store water between their leaves. When the larvae are born, the female carries them on her back to separate locations to facilitate their survival. She will visit them and deposit infertile eggs that they feed on until they complete metamorphosis.

Horned marsupial frog
Gastrotheca cornuta

Sumaco horned treefrog
Hemiphractus proboscideus

MARSUPIAL FROGS

The South American horned marsupial frog lays fertilised eggs in pouches located on the frog's back. Once they have fully developed, the hatchlings emerge from the pouch.

SUPER MUM

The female Sumaco horned treefrog carries her eggs on her back, keeping them safe as they grow.

Spectacled caiman
Caiman crocodilus

GOOD MOTHERS

Crocodiles make nests in which to lay their eggs. In some species, like the spectacled caiman, the mothers care for their eggs and young until they grow up and are ready to hunt on their own.

Golden poison frog
Phyllobates terribilis

DEDICATED FATHERS

Some South American frogs lay their eggs on top of leaves, where the male watches over them. When they are born, the tadpoles climb onto their father's back. The father carries them to small puddles where they are released and continue to feed until they grow up.

Green sea turtle
Chelonia mydas

Hatchlings

INCREDIBLE JOURNEY

Sea turtles travel very far to lay their eggs, going back to the same beach on which they were born. The females emerge from the sea and deposit their eggs in a nest, cover them with sand and then leave. When the babies hatch all alone, they use moonlight to find the ocean while trying to avoid predators.

DEFENCE AND ADAPTATION

Living creatures use different strategies to survive, adapt to their environment and to defend themselves against other animals. Amphibians and reptiles have developed extraordinary and diverse strategies for defence and adaptation.

DETACHABLE TAIL

Some reptiles automatically amputate their tail to distract their predator and escape. Afterwards, a new tail grows in its place. This is called caudal autotomy and can happen several times throughout their life.

Western skink
Eumeces skiltonianus

The severed tail continues to wiggle for a while

VENOMOUS SNAKES

The main purpose of venom is to kill a snake's prey, but it can also be used as a defence.

Eastern diamondback rattlesnake
Crotalus adamanteus

Greater siren
Siren lacertina

WAITING PATIENTLY

When the atmosphere is too dry, the greater siren buries itself under mud, becoming dormant until the rain returns.

NO SALT, PLEASE

The marine iguana lives in salt water, but ingesting too much salt can be dangerous. Through adaptation, salt is filtered from its blood and expelled through a special nasal gland.

Marine iguana
Amblyrhynchus cristatus

Arrau turtle
Podocnemis expansa

AVOIDING PROBLEMS

Turtles protect themselves by hiding their legs, neck and head in their shell.

CAMOUFLAGE

Camouflage consists of mimicking and blending in with the environment. It is the first line of defence for many amphibians and reptiles. They use their colouring and shape to appear like a part of nature. The American green tree frog, for example, mimics leaves.

American green tree frog
Dryophytes cinereus

DON'T MESS WITH ME!

Toads inflate their lungs and raise their limbs to appear larger than they are.

SALAMANDER STRATEGIES

Some species of salamanders whip their tails and others have toxic glands that they use to defend themselves from predators.

Eastern newt
Notophthalmus viridescens

Gila monster
Heloderma suspectum

Eastern diamondback rattlesnake
Crotalus adamanteus

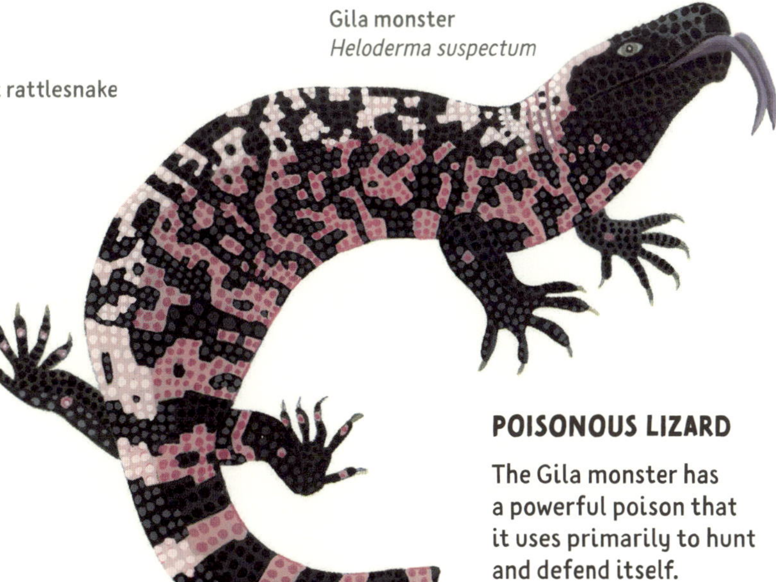

WARNINGS

The eastern diamondback rattlesnake uses its rattle to scare away its predators. Other snakes poo to defend themselves.

POISONOUS LIZARD

The Gila monster has a powerful poison that it uses primarily to hunt and defend itself.

Golden poison frog
Phyllobates terribilis

BRIGHT COLOURS

Frogs like the golden poison frog or the strawberry poison-dart frog have bright colours to show they are poisonous, so animals avoid them. Other species have striking colours to mimic being poisonous, even though they aren't.

Strawberry poison-dart frog
Oophaga pumilio

DECEPTION

As one of their defence mechanisms, Darwin's frog and fire-bellied toads show their underside, which has different colours and patterns, warning their predators.

Cuyaba dwarf frog
Physalaemus nattereri

Darwin's frog
Rhinoderma darwinii

HIND-SIGHT

The Cuyaba dwarf frog has markings on its back that resemble two eyes, which it uses to startle predators.

Texas horned lizard
Phrynosoma cornutum

Eastern hog-nosed snake
Heterodon platirhinos

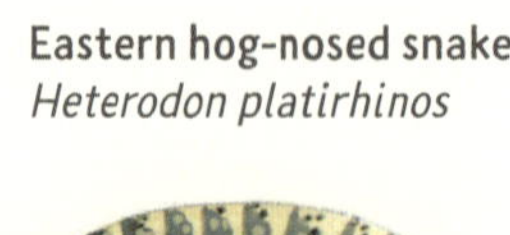

PLAYING DEAD

Many amphibians and reptiles stay still, curl up or flip over so that their attackers believe they are dead and do not harm them. The hog-nosed snake even sticks out its tongue to make its act more convincing.

RUNNING ON WATER

The common basilisk is an agile lizard that can run across water thanks to its incredible speed and unique hind legs.

Common basilisk
Basiliscus basiliscus

Its hind legs have flaps of skin on the toes that act like fins, increasing the surface area of the foot.

Texas horned lizard
Phrynosoma cornutum

CRYING BLOOD

The Texas horned lizard fills its lungs with air to appear bigger and avoid being eaten. If this isn't enough, it also opens its mouth, whistles and spurts blood out of its eyes!

Atacama toad
Rhinella atacamensis

AMAZING SURVIVOR

The Atacama toad is the only amphibian that has managed to survive and colonise the Atacama Desert in Chile, the driest desert in the world.

CONSERVATION

In an increasingly complex world, it is difficult to know what to do to save species from extinction. Breeding centres have been set up to rescue species that cannot be saved in the wild. They face many risks, so it's important to learn about these species, value them and care for them.

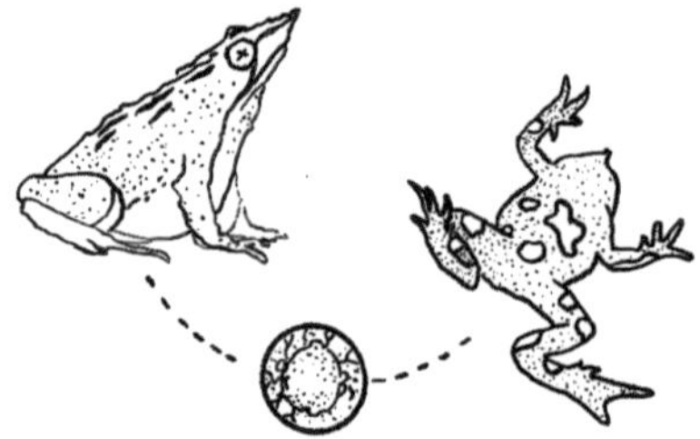    

ILLNESSES

Some fungi spread easily among amphibians and reptiles, and they don't always have protection against these diseases.

FASHION

Various crocodiles, boas, pythons and lizards are widely hunted for their skin to make shoes, boots, bags, belts and more. Many are also eaten by humans, like some turtles and frogs. Other species, like the red-footed tortoise, are hunted to make medicine.

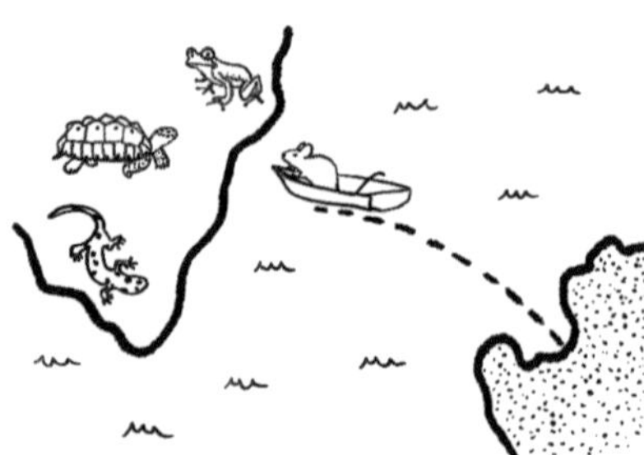  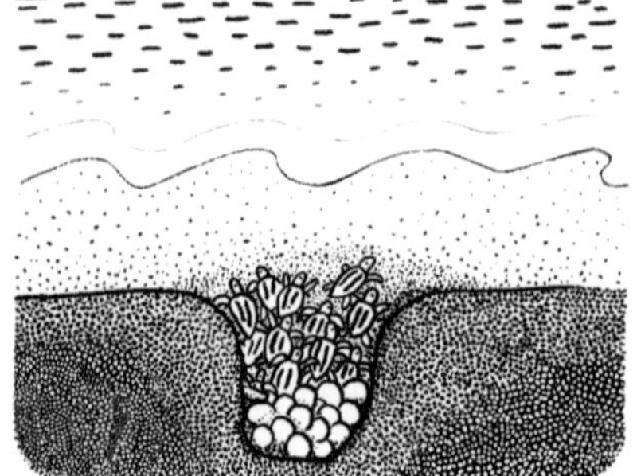

NON-NATIVE SPECIES

Introduced species can harm native amphibians and reptiles. For example, rats accidentally introduced to the Galápagos Islands eat turtle eggs and hatchlings.

CLIMATE CHANGE

Warmer temperatures impact amphibians and reptiles in many ways. They can change where these animals live, when they breed or hibernate, and even the number of males and females born, since temperature affects egg development.

  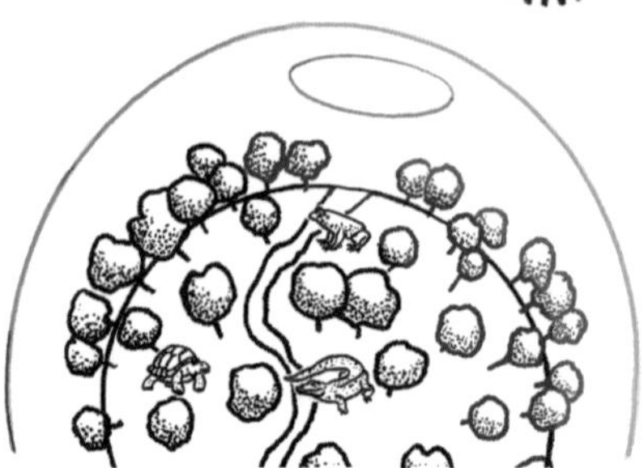

LOSS OF HABITAT

Growing cities, agriculture, pollution and deforestation destroy many species' habitats.

ULTRAVIOLET RADIATION

The depletion of the ozone layer, and the resulting increase in radiation, has many different effects. It negatively impacts thermoregulation and harms larvae that have no protection against radiation.

Many of these factors interact with each other and affect these animals' lives.

HOW CAN YOU HELP?

There are many ways each of us can help the world become a better place for amphibians and reptiles, and all other animals.

WHAT YOU SHOULD AVOID:

If you move a stone or log to look for animals, always put it back – it might be their shelter. Protect their homes!

Don't keep wild amphibians and reptiles as pets – watch them in nature instead! Taking them from the wild is illegal for some species. If you want a pet reptile or amphibian, choose a captive-bred one from a licensed breeder.

Never release non-native amphibians or reptiles into the wild. They might harm local species by eating them or competing for food and space.

Avoid products made from amphibians or reptiles, and don't eat them. The less we use them, the more lives we save.

WHAT YOU CAN DO:

Read about reptiles and amphibians. This way, you can learn about these animals, appreciate them and try to protect them.

Volunteer for a charity or project that protects them. Ask an adult to help you find opportunities nearby. You could help animals cross roads safely or assist in tracking their populations.

Share your interest in protecting these animals. Explain just how important they are to your friends, relatives and classmates.

Transform your house and surrounding areas by leaving fallen leaves, rocks and logs on the ground so that amphibians and reptiles have shelter.

FURTHER READING AND RESOURCES

Below are three exemplary organisations whose
work helps protect amphibians and reptiles.

Save the Frogs
Since 2008, this organisation has carried out more
than 2,000 educational events in 57 countries to
inspire, educate and empower people to protect
amphibians. Save the Frogs members also focus
on creating and restoring habitats for threatened
amphibian populations.

Turtle Survival Alliance
The Turtle Survival Alliance helps protect endangered turtles
through research, education, and rescue programmes. In Belize
and Colombia, they raise baby turtles in safe environments and
release them when they are big enough to avoid predators.

The Amphibian and Reptile Conservation Trust
The Amphibian and Reptile Conservation Trust (ARC) is a British
charity dedicated to protecting the UK's frogs, toads, newts,
snakes and lizards. They conduct research on these animals and
their habitats, manage over 80 nature reserves, and engage
local communities in conservation efforts. ARC offers workshops,
training, and educational programs for schools and other groups
to raise awareness and promote the protection of these species.

Smooth helmeted iguana
Corytophanes cristatus

CONSERVATIONIST ORGANISATIONS
AND WEBSITES

> **Amphibian Ark** > www.amphibianark.org
> **Amphibian and Reptile Conservancy** > www.amphibianandreptileconservancy.org
> **Conservation International** > www.conservation.org
> **International Reptile Conservation Foundation** > www.ircf.org
> **Kids Saving The Rainforest** > www.kidssavingtherainforest.org
> **Partners in Amphibian and Reptile Conservation** > www.parcplace.org
> **Paso Pacifico** > www.pasopacifico.org
> **Save the Frogs** > www.savethefrogs.com
> **Sea Turtle Conservancy** > www.conserveturtles.org
> **The Amphibian and Reptile Conservation Trust** > www.arc-trust.org
> **The Nature Conservancy** > www.nature.org
> **Turtle Survival Alliance** > www.turtlesurvival.org

GLOSSARY

Amniote: A vertebrate whose embryos develop inside four special membranes, providing protection and nutrients.

Amplexus: The mating position in amphibians, where the male holds onto the female's back to reproduce.

Anatomy: The structure of a living being and how its body parts are arranged.

Caudal autotomy: A defence strategy where an animal detaches a limb or tail to escape from a predator.

Carboniferous: A geological period, around 359–299 million years ago, when the first reptiles appeared, and amphibians thrived in swampy forests.

Devonian: A geological era, about 365 million years ago, when the first amphibians appeared. These fish-like creatures with lobed fins were ancestors of all four-limbed vertebrates, including dinosaurs and mammals.

Ecosystem: A community of living things in a certain area that interact with each other and their surroundings.

Ectotherm: An animal that cannot produce its own body heat and relies on the environment to stay warm.

Evolutionary tree: A diagram that shows how different species are related through evolution.

Extinction: When all members of an animal or plant species disappear forever. This can happen in one place or worldwide.

Gills: Breathing organs in fish and other water animals, usually found on the sides of the head. Gills absorb oxygen from water so the animal can breathe.

Habitat: The natural home of an animal, where it finds air, water, food and shelter. This can be a forest, lake, desert or even a tree trunk.

Life cycle: The stages an organism goes through from birth to death.

Lissamphibia: A group of modern amphibians, including frogs, toads, salamanders and caecilians.

Metamorphosis: A big change in an animal's body as it grows, affecting how it looks and lives.

Moulting: When an animal sheds and replaces old skin with new skin.

Oviparous: Animals that lay eggs, like birds, reptiles, amphibians, and some sea creatures.

Permian: A geological period, around 299–252 million years ago, when reptiles became more dominant, and many early amphibians went extinct.

Reproduction: The process by which living things create new life.

Tetrapod: A vertebrate with four limbs, including mammals, amphibians, birds, and reptiles.

Thermoregulation: How animals control their body temperature to stay healthy, even when the weather changes.

Viviparous: Animals that give birth to live young, like most mammals.

Golden toad
Incilius periglenes

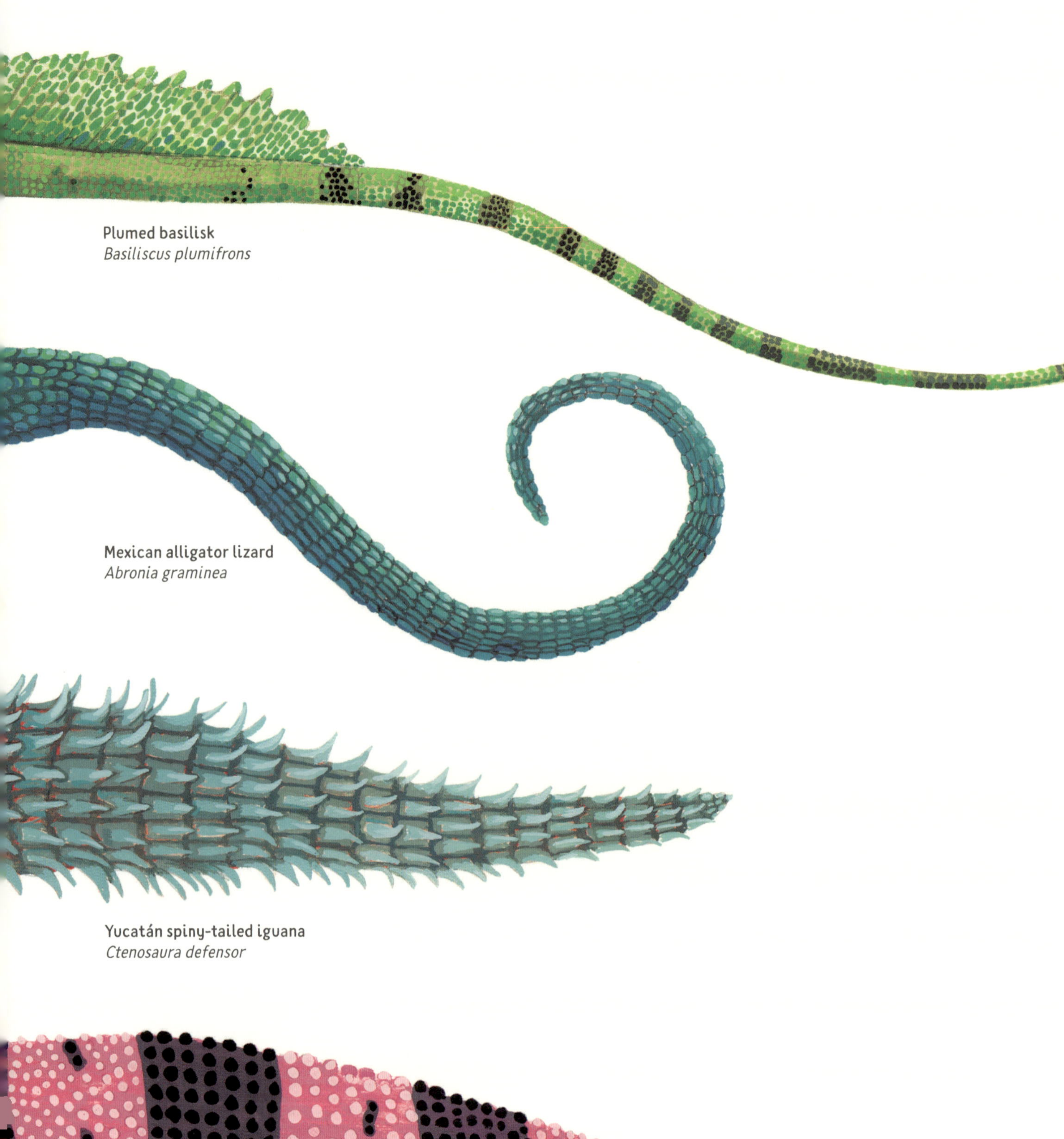

Plumed basilisk
Basiliscus plumifrons

Mexican alligator lizard
Abronia graminea

Yucatán spiny-tailed iguana
Ctenosaura defensor

Gila monster
Heloderma suspectum

BIBLIOGRAPHY

Angulo A., Rueda-Almonacid J. V., Rodríguez-Mahecha J. V. and La Marca E. (2006). 'Técnicas de inventario y monitoreo para los anfibios de la región tropical andina' [Inventory and monitoring techniques for amphibians of the tropical Andean region], *Serie Manuales de Campo No2*. Conservación Internacional. Panamericana Formas e Impresos S.A., Bogotá D.C. pg. 298.

Charrier A., Correa C., Castro C. and Méndez M., (2015). 'A new species of Alsodes (Anura: Alsodidae) from Altos de Cantillana, Central Chile', *Zootaxa 3915* (4): 540–550.

Charrier A., Mora M., Correa C. and Palma E. (2017). *Monitoreo y Conservación de Anfibios Alto Andinos de la Región Metropolitana* [Monitoring and Conservation of High Andean Amphibians in the Metropolitan Region]. pg. 83.

Charrier A. (2021). *Croares: Concierto a cielo abierto* [Croaks: An Open-Air Concert]. Zapallar, Chile: Editorial Manivela. pg. 11.

Crump M. (2000). *In Search of the Golden Frog.* Chicago, IL: University of Chicago Press. pg. 320.

Crump M. (2010). *Mysteries of the Komodo Dragon: The Biggest, Deadliest Lizard Gives Up Its Secrets.* Honesdale, PA: Boyds Mills Press. pg. 40.

Crump M. (2011). *Amphibians and Reptiles: An Introduction to their Natural History and Conservation.* Granville, OH: McDonald & Woodward Publishing. pg. 280.

Crump M. (2013). *The Mystery of Darwin's Frog.* Honesdale, PA: Boyds Mills Press. pg. 40.

Crump M. (2015). *Eye of Newt and Toe of Frog, Adder's Fork and Lizard's Leg: The Lore and Mythology of Amphibians and Reptiles.* Chicago, IL: University of Chicago Press. pg. 304.

Crump M. (2018). *A Year with Nature: An Almanac.* Chicago, IL: University of Chicago Press. pg. 384.

Duméril A. & Bibron G. (1841). *Erpétologie générale ou histoire naturelle complete des reptiles [General Herpetology, or the Complete Natural History of Reptiles].* Librairie Encyclopédique de Roret, Paris. pg. 488.

Díaz-Páez H., Núñez J. J., Núñez H. and Ortiz J. C. (2008). 'Estado de conservación de anfibios y reptiles' [Conservation status of amphibians and reptiles], *Herpetología de Chile.* eds. Vidal M.A. and Labra A. Science Verlag, Santiago. pg 233–267.

Pough F. H., Andrews R. M., Crump M. L., Savitzky A. H., Wells K. D. and Brandley M. C. (2016). *Herpetology* (fourth edition). Sunderland, MA: Sinauer Associates, Inc. pg. 591.

Fenolio D., Fabry M., Charrier A., Tirado M., Crump M. and Lamar B. (2012). 'The Darwin's Frog Conservation Initiative'. *Leaf Litter* 4(1): 11–17.

Fenolio D. B., Moreno-Puig V., Levy M. G., Núñez J. J., Lamar W. W., Fabry M. O., Tirado M. S., Crump M. and Charrier A. (2013). 'Status and Conservation of a Gondwana Legacy: Bullock's False Toad, Telmatobufo bullocki (Amphibia: Anura: Calyptocephalellidae)'. *Herpetological Review* 44(4): 583–590.

Jiménez de la Espada D. M. (1872). 'Sobre la reproducción de *Rhinoderma darwinii*' [On the reproduction of *Rhinoderma dawinii*]. *Anales de la Sociedad Española de Historia Natural* 1: 139–155.

Philippi R. A. (1902). *Suplemento a los Batraquios Chilenos Descritos en la Historia Física i Política de Chile de don Claudio Gay* [Supplement to the Chilean Batrachians described in the Physical and Political History of Chile by Claudio Gay]/ Librería Ivens. Santiago, Chile. pg. xi, 160.

Young B. E., Stuart J. S., Chanson N. A. Cox A. T. & Boucher T. M. (2004). *Disappearing Jewels: The Status of New World Amphibians.* NatureServe, Arlington, Virginia. pg. 60.